You-Valuism: The Scripture

Benjamin De Silva

chipmunkapublishing
the mental health publisher

Benjamin De Silva

Published by
Chipmunkapublishing
United Kingdom

http://www.chipmunkapublishing.com

Copyright © Ishara de Silva 2018

ISBN   978-1-78382-441-0

AUTHOR BIOGRAPHY

*I was born in Sri Lanka, Kandy, in 1971, during a time of great
internal strife on the island. My parents, both university educated,
came to London in 1973 when I was two years old. We lived in
North London, a rough area known as Archway and attended St
John's primary school. My father was a socialist so we were not
isolated Asians, but integrated strongly with the white community.
I was very sporty and won every race on sports day except the egg
and spoon and mixed with people who lived close by. After
primary school, I went to secondary school in Tufnell Park but
didn't get the grades to go to university so continued my education
at sixth form college.*

*A late starter, by 25, I went to SOAS, the School of Oriental and
African Studies, where I studied two years of a political studies
degree before my illness struck.*

*I was sitting in the common room when suddenly I could hear
voices. I responded to them in my own mind. I went home and was
reading Hegel when suddenly a voice shouted out "lie". There
were eventually four voices all shouting slogans at me. I went to
my mother's house and asked her if she could hear anything. She
said no. When I said I could hear some voices, she called my
brother in a panic.*

*He came round and massaged me, and the next day I was taken to
the doctors. They said I would never recover and put me on
medication. A few years later, I started working on a newspaper
set up by my dad in conjunction with others and later went on to
edit a national paper, The Asian Times, with voices ploughing in
my head disturbingly.*

*After Asian Times, I was still feeling the heat of schizophrenia and
allowed my place and physical appearance to go down.
Eventually, some police and social workers came around and said
they were taking me to a mental hospital.*

*I spent three months in involuntary detention at London's St
Anne's mental health hospital after I was released. I went on to
write this book using the voices of schizophrenia. A large
proportion of this book was dictated by voices even though the
idea in it - that of a selfless politics – was rationally produced.
One of the articles, on a world military, is based on the use of
visual data meditation, perhaps, The Divine Eye, in Buddhism, not
sure, and was published in Ceylon Today, a national paper,*

online, in Sri Lanka, but it is unclear whether the voices of schizophrenia interfered with the result or not. Maybe it was just an aid which can see the data in-mind accurately. Sounds good? Much of this work is careful, even though auditory voices – external or internal – produced it, but there are some segments which defy logic and are incomprehensible or at least challenging to the reader, which have been left in for authenticity. Still, the general bulk of the book holds true. And even the editing was helped by the voices themselves, for good or not so good. You judge!!

The manuscript is calling for a new politics of selflessness, something which I call You-Valuism, and, surprisingly, the voices of schizophrenia could work to this theme miraculously, knowing strong past-related and new insights related to this notion, even if I pre-empted the position of clause, not the outcome, fully. Hopefully, this book will provide fresh insights into so-called schizophrenic "hallucinations" and help contribute to medical history in a way that offers hope as to <u>whether Schizophrenia is an evolutionary advantage such as the Divine Ear as some Buddhists hold or a biological or chemical defect like the west envisage.</u> What follows, by and large, including the introduction is what the voices told me....except for a number of articles by me published in Sri Lankan media which have been interwoven into the theme for a happier ride!

YOU-VALUISM:
The idea of a schizophrenic

Benjamin De Silva

Intro

The term You-Valuism is not an ideology, it's a shown agenda, not only prone to realisation in the South Asia brown colour, but a hoped for dream for mankind. So who won? The LTTE or the Sri Lankan government? Neither! Both lost in numbers and in spirituality. Let's have a higher dream that beats Communism and Nationalism, not only Capitalism, not only in South Asia, but the world over, for a You-Valuist agenda like Socialism, but, well, not quite.

Put simply, it is the love of selflessness. Not dodgy Anything Goesism, not unlike crime but further afield, which sees all of life as meaningless, so no responsibility, primarily, for our actions, at start. Well, the world does have meaning, according to You-Valuism, and it's steeper than Marx, only closer to Gandhi, well not quite, again. Mainly because it's not in opposition to anyone. No war can be fought in the name of You-value ethics, because it's against its principles. That's how India won, even if Sri Lanka was its servant.

But You-Valuism, again, is a world dream for man, and woman, which sees people as people, not as servants. Yes we can win, and society is heading that way, with the brown colour in to benefit the dream's pinnacle and spearhead it to victory, we see. The brown community, yes globally, can help steer it, hopefully, to a no loss, yes we can, again, ensure that You-Valuism does not lose, because it was the dream, selflessness, of Gandhi and Buddha, and is the pinnacle of all religions in the South Asia region.

Importing it abroad may take time, but it is not useless. Nor will it be, if the production system and finance, not just society, are allowed to function in a You-Valuist way, by linking it not to profit or investment, but need, like Marx, freely given, without money wishing for more desire added on, with a suffering to match.

Yes, it's an 'all for all' system, not one for all, like in the three musketeers, and can survive any blackout, with a will to defeat anything lower if it succumbs to more selfishness and greed, something everyone is capable of, regardless of race or creed. We can win. We will win. We must win. Even if we need world Socialism first, to overcome the work pace.

You-Valuism isn't over with random acts of selflessness. That's just the beginning. It can move to unlimited selfless acts to others and oneself, until all bleeds in healthily mind-wise, so is linked to mental health and ease. It is the world over, a need to return to a healthy state of mind, for everyone, which is accompanied in western and eastern psychology, but not all see selflessness as its goal. Well, Buddhism does. And we can win.

The primary objective of the You-Valuist drive is to see unlimited capacity for selfless acts multiply until all is revolving around compassion and kindness to all, so lets not tumble and make a mess, because You-Valuism is the way of religion, where religion and politics can mix well, until all blends into a stateless world because all is compassionate all round, a real heaven right here, on Earth, slim and fine, until it breeds no wrath and can sit comfortably with its own warrant for the end of greed, hatred and delusion, the Buddhist dream for Earth!

The Enlightenment: That a stage beyond Communism exists, mainly politically, which manifests most commonly in the literature of South Asia of brown colour, an enlightenment that paves the way for a You-Value society and polity globally that will lead the way to a brighter world where selflessly driven individuals replace the climate of hostility that permeates the world today.

The limits of political philosophy!

So, not so strong! Let's win. The You-Value guise is on, without horrid or trouble. Yes, Marx wanted a cooperative world, with less competitive in, which he said caused, the chase after money, all wars and colonialism as the peak. But should we peak it, or change it!? Yes, Buddhists say change is what we should focus on, not peaks and troughs, for better adaptability.

But You-Valuism is a peak, the highest order of the polity, but we can change to it! So let's not grumble. One day, we will win!! But don't over trough, or get depressed, because it's not that far off. We already have one fifth of the world's population, or there abouts, in brown skin colour, in South Asia, taking the toll, like it did under Colonialism, to win its original tradition and history which the whites, now not so unruly, stole.

Let's not quibble about vengeance. The whites and westerners are on a learning game also, and we should forgive, because suffering unleashed is suffering within, so we all know they are, one day, on their way to higher freedom and happy, if they comply.

The day will come when all political philosophy is on a You-Value spirit, a selfless abode, where no one gripes anymore, and all is still, without needing to hide or wonder what the Earth was like, one day.

Let's forgive. The westerners weren't all wrong, but they lost their way and can recover and have marvellous philosophy to warrant a higher education superior to much of the world, well maybe. Even Oxford wasn't all full of toffs when Marx was around, because the socialists wanted a fairer world order and a world military, which we proposed, is a need, not of the hour, but of the day at least!

So don't worry. We're all in strong, with You-Valuism at the peak, ruling out wash it away or unruly behaviour because one day there will be no need for demonstrations and knock offs, because we're all winning when You-Valuism materialises or gets its way.

Existentialism, on the one hand, isn't systemic but a persona, but let's keep it neat. It still says life is meaningless, and capitalism says we want it for ourselves. Only Marx said, in crux, that it should be transcended with an 'us' for cooperation. But it stops there, in political philosophy with Hobbes classed as a liberal, but staying in a state of nature, where Existentialism picks up from. But that won't do. Much of the global population is encouraged, in scriptures, to be selfless, which is beyond all of this. So we need to comply whole heartedly. This is where it's at! The 'You' in selflessness, untouched in political philosophy, not even Gramsci with 'Hegemony' touched on it, and it leaves a bare mark in society and political life.

Adam Smith stuck to Capitalism, and the less sombre political theorists stayed away. Not even in South Asia has it materialised as a philosophy beyond the religions, into politics. So this is where we should stick! You-Valuism is the key, unseen in political theory, so far. Not a prescription, but a reality. Let's comply! Unless, and only if, there is too much horror in our way, whether personal or in the polity. Yes.

The Way In 2 a You-Value polity!

The need is in. For a You-Value polity of selflessness and grace, without horror in, trickled down to all services and institutions, including and incorporating mental health and the doctors surgery, and wider afield, until all is clear, again, not unneat.

The Way In philosophy to 'you' is simple: A 'no value' polity/society, to a 'me value' polity, to an 'us value' polity, to a 'you value' polity of selflessness and non-greed.

And this is where we should stick. This the reason we should live more service-driven and reasonable livings, with little ambivalence and a tolerant outlook, so all is not uncanny and bizarre, like a Colombo episode, of the police superintendent who cunningly catches stupefied criminals in the knees, like all families can become with so much inadvertency in.

So let's keep care in, with all this bonanza to life, so the polity can mature to fruition, with less strife and wrangle, and more kindliness and caringness near us, all the way to a You-Value polity which encourages us on without no no care, because negation isn't the way, here, like Marx explained, but 'the solution to the solution' is how we should add on, not back track uncannily. Both the west and east have good qualities like generosity in the former and service-kinds in the latter, so let's keep it up and get prim and proper so all is well-managed and we no longer have to fear death at the hands of others.

Can the Deathless be true, the idea that we "not die" rather than "add on" life eternally? But what would society think if some people still have to die with it in? Let's not worry about over-taboo, because the general picture is bleak anyway, if Earth life was a former hell before non-culprits like Buddha and Christ came in, and the top philosophers!

South Asia may have a better chance of the deathless, which means no murders or vengeance, even in hospitals or mental health clinics, no, institutions. But that doesn't mean everyone doesn't die. Perhaps, the life energy system gets cut off if we are left alone, but society still has to comply. But what if it doesn't get cut off?

Society without a guise needs a 'you' both-ways, not just in the polity, but in society as well, ideally. It takes two to tango, as they say. So lest keep it ungrim and make a start with it. Live and let live. Let's ban age limits in society so the bank, or dole queue, or even at work, isn't stopped from keeping people on even after retirement, however long, even for eternal beings who pop up once in a while.

But the West should follow too, where there is less speak of eternity in literature, sacred, on Earth maybe, and Africa and the Orient. Let's bless life and make any age limit the target, whether there is murder, which there is, or not. Let's cut off the worry, and the police will follow. That's not to say we shouldn't add life, too, only that a You-Value society is a prerequisite for change, for more eternity and scope, scientifically or not, or just with the advancement of the evolution of spiritual power.

So, let's follow and make it 'you', quickly, and surely, not fast and dangerously, until all can live on whatever age they are, however far off, even up to the 600 years of age mark or beyond, if spiritual upkeep make it possible with eternal beings in the pipe. The political leaders should make the start, and let it go on, in legislation, even limitless. So let's begin!! And make a swing of it.

Spying &The You-Value Game

Don't quit. The spying games have reached maximum overload and you'll see it everywhere you look, in your street, in the subway, at work. But don't stupefy. The six sense base, which might allow it in isn't trim and covers the mind in delusion, if, and when, there are more causes to an event, than the individual sense pick up used by the six sense game allows.

Yes, we're in a deluded world like the Buddha comprehended and the sixth sense only lets you off a little but not all the way, because all is still on a negative and can't get its way. So be still. And let it wither away. Focus on what you need, mainly, not want, and let it creep in, is The Buddhist Way in Zen at least and other eastern traditions.

Lest creep to our win without creepy but all on a no loose, which is our win. Like the South Asians tried to do after and during colonialism, but not all the way. The post-colonial period was reaped in a "getaway" and succumbed to western pressure, where all the Buddhist books had to be returned, for one, to Sri Lanka and a Burmese monk brought in to replace the long standing tradition of Buddhism with a re-cultivation of the religion after the British dismantled it.

Spying is wrong and it is understandable, both at the same time. So we've got to create the conditions for it to ripe lesser and regalvanate a wiser approach to fending off inadvertency and recapture a worldly spirit which no longer washes in a domineering hegemonic role for us ever.

Yes, blocking through spying in the West or speaking our senses to others even when silent outside to you, is a toll that requires us to spoon feed wrath which is no longer required if we take it on with a wiser affordable non-antagoniser which can benefit us all.

Is this the frequent way until you win? To block. Let's hope not, because the colonial era of the past has to come to a close with a wider look at our militaries and strategy focus so all can live as one, one day, and can all speak of a higher spirituality that reaps no reward for one or the few but for everyone everywhere.

Divide and rule tactics must come to an end, to divide families (and expansiveness and stretching strategy as, we see, with Muslims second and South Asia prior), and let's hope South Asia doesn't follow suit with the sense syndrome of spying unless it warrants an intelligentsia focus which is required only in danger. But not otherwise. We have to win. Until all is reaping a higher morality and life can begin without fear or scorn for us all.

South Asia can lead the way by focusing on what you need and can have, rather than on what's near for a jeopardising persona which leads others to betray, because we are all the wiser for loving one another and leading on a no dig until all is clear for us all, a return to normalcy and world peace.

That way, the militaries of the world can realign to a higher truth which is beneficial for us all, where the world-earth map is the reamed for persona on a less inclined to affray, so that each country retains its national independence but works together to keep the sum total of militaries at bay. In this sense, the wider way, without horror in, we can work to reduce the spying game until all is soothed and smoothed in time and everyone gets their way.

Formalising a world military

It is not unknown for militaries to war, formally or informally, and Russia is on the brink of Ukraine. Let's hope, not willow. Because all is on a top notch account if all wise in to utopia. The idea of a world military to end war, a much publicised idea, not now, maybe, but in the future. So can it work, or should it enact a new debate on the heralding world military line up?

Let's see. But don't despair, all is not lost with Russia having prepared fighter jets for the go. Not star wars, but space wars, are on the war accounting agenda. Or have been. But where will it lead, if we can't stop the fighting here on Earth?

The military is a typical conundrum. Not a rook, but a Westphalia set up for a treaty that lost its way. Let's inside, not insider, be. Just be! Because that's the philosophy we need to stop attacking and retry for a higher run.

China tops the target list in the US. But latest revelations show it is modernising. What a tyrant, you say, or can it decipher the meaning of "wanna be on your way", because all its philosophy is geared on "the way to go", some say. So let's cherish it.

Confucius and others, in Orient, are known for their way and war theory. And Bruce Lee, on a more streetwise level, tops the board. But how can culture, philosophically, higher up, that has torched war as a "go", be its instigator? Or can it? Maybe we're being over cautious. But a world military, with china on board, warrants a way that is not a go, but a stop. A stop or end to war, like the UN, but better.

The idea, a world military saga, touched on, in a meditation in Sri Lanka's leading online newspaper, Ceylon Today, proclaimed a world military is, or ought be, on the cards. So it can non-run, and Russia needn't falter.

Barack Obama had the right idea when he said, in one review, that he wanted to speak of a time when the war in Afghanistan can come to a successful conclusion. Well now it must, fully, even after troops withdrawn, not unsung with protests for it, but a tightly lit, professional overtone, to each state to ensure successful conclusion of the one world army concept, once all clears, however long the process, even decades, if not centuries away.

The writer of that review, in an unknown, to me, title, however, claimed that strategy in conflict is changing, so much so, that we cannot make meaning, again, of the reasoning behind the definitions of war in the modern "armed struggle" sub-state types, we envisage.

But can we? Not necessary. The extended current period need not be a war fiasco, and when it ends, eventually, all we need to cult out, commonly, not demonstrably, but through personal conviction, each one of us, is what could be described as "dovish". A dove of peace, that takes us on to a higher reality here, on our premises, home ground, not away to a distant far off galaxy.

So rest assured, Obama, that, most say, in One World land, that wars are not over for one reason, both intra, internally, and outer, between nations. Namely, because we yet to reveal, among us, starting from within, a shared history of oneness. We need unification instead of non-calmness. So shall we just be, globally and in polity, world-wide, and see if a world military stops, one day, the toll; where all can live peacefully and as one? Let's not shy away and dare once all else fails.

Ethnic Groups: Not too slow, only slower!

A limited number, not a minority number, of ethnics!, is how to break the ice. Then you know we're not there to scare you, but to sleep comfortably, not too long though, if work helps us overcome bad karma, on an all get to "You", not an "I" or "Me", "Us", eventually – which makes Earth selfless. That's where added power adds on happier! Brown is closer selflessly-wise, but that doesn't make it better! There's still a long way to go, since the Buddha came in over 2500 years ago, so let's still try, even with all the rebirth in, all the way through.

Now that's a clever route, that's when we know we're not wrong, or do you?, not a space-time reality, all the way, only in time, because that's where space is, not to be unsure. Keep it within, internal, not just intrinsic, and essential all the way to a clever bank, not sky high, but Earthed, all the way, deep-rooted, nice, and calm. Then you know that we're here, the Buddhist non-trough, which offers kindness in the here and now which is where ethnics fly to when all goes wrong, which it is.

Keep it ongoing, to avoid the wrath and stay with calmness, rather than transform or time-travel, Steve McQueeny, all a bet. Transforms can laugh on, but what's the bet, to outsmart or compliment? Let's say compliment? So, who is Buddhist monk Ajahn Sumedho, a laugh on, or a grammar queen? Joke. With respect, Sumedho. He's Neither. He's our best, and I like or try to be nice to myself and him. So let's not bother wrongly, if he's our best bet. Investigation is the best, so do it. Or not bother? Even the Sangha, the Buddhist ring, which is our best option, do, so stay steady, and not rock and roll. Calmly.

Now you know how to try. Or is it, like a clever Rhino in the wild, who stays slim, but thick, to avoid aggression to its own tribe - flowers do it. Which just walk, no let's not blow it, because they are higher up in the animal, not human kingdom, where Earth took off, before animal, or is it? So, is it a higher lower, the human to animal species link, we say lower in animal but the wrong way in, if humans were first? Maybe, maybe not. Hobbes anticipated unfair, and animal can be seen in man, which is the correct Kung Fu hook, I see, at least, for fairer, so everyone can wonder if Rebirth is in!

Now no no nice ethnic minorities, so which is cleverer?!

A limited number, or, a minority number of ethnics in other countries, including South Asia (brown or black), over Rebirth?, let's say, to cover with no inadvertency.

I see, higher enlightenment heather in the limited number stake.

You-Valuism

In a previous article in the Sri Lanka Guardian, not so long ago, I said that a You-value movement in South Asia, just like the Non-Aligned Movement, there, would be good for the region and prove to be a leadership success that tallies with the strength of religions in South Asia like Hinduism and Buddhism, not to mention Islam, but not ruling out other, western, religions, too.

"You-Valuism" is a term I've coined to describe You-value ethics like compassion and altruistic love but in a political context, not just religious. It is a step after Existentialism's "anything goes" attitude, Capitalism's "Me-value" approach of getting what I can for me, Socialism's "Us-value" credentials of cooperation, nationalisation and other "communal" endeavor's – to the You-value form of selfless giving.

Karl Marx, in part, came to his views by relying on early Communes which were a more primitive form of Communism which he said resembled the basis for a global Communism in future where the technological forces of mankind would be unleashed in a way that benefits all.

Whatever! The question is: Can we see an even higher form of society based on studying the religious forms, primitive and modern, rather than the Paris Commune, to see an even higher foundation for the progress of societies, world-wide, in time to come? And can, or will it take, a political form also? – including in the West.

Despite their divisions, the You-value ethics of all pure religions is what binds them despite their differences into a common bond, something, virtue that is, that virtually all leading philosophers recommended as the source of happiness in this life – in both east and west.

I have wrote, in a previous article, that mind may be evolving from binary good/bad, to unitary just good, and finally to Zero: emptiness, peace and the knower's mind (near self-realisation), and that this evolution may reveal how we might get there – to a stage of You-Valuism, that is.

So, could You-Valuist political movements exist or develop, just like the other socialist or capitalist parties – either in South Asia, or internationally? What would this mean, economically? Is generosity the real cause of wealth as at least one religion insists? Who would they represent? Everyone, or not? What would be their methodology?: democracy, revolution, or, as I think, Compassion.

As one religion once, to paraphrase, said: "Those who commit suffering on you do so because they themselves are suffering. What they need is help, not punishment."

So is You-Valuism a valid alternative? I think so.

Virtue and politics can mix.

The need for wisdom in the world is self-evident. As Ajahn Sumedho, retired abbot of Amaravati Buddhist monastery, in Hemel Hempstead, England, has explained: "We cannot really create a true democracy or a true communism or a true socialism – we cannot create that because we are still deluded by a sense of self. So it ends up in tyranny and in selfishness, fear and suspicion."

You-Valuism, on the other hand, is liberation from the "normal" sense of ordinary Self of a personality type so selfless and so leans towards the cultivation of a truly selfless political system and attitude to the world.

I'll leave it there……for now.

You-Valuism for South Asia (Brown)

Eradicating poverty may be useless in some modes of production. But You-Valuism is selfless, which is one up on a Me-value capitalism, or an Us-value communism, which makes it a hunger less mode of production for "all get all", without worry of starvation, devoid of a meaningless existence in a no suicide drive. So let's make, no let it happen! Let's make it win. Without hurry or revolution. Let's beat the Marxism of the past, and let it all go ahead unwildly, but ungrim too, to unnoose it, and let it be! Live Aid may be it, but You-Valuism tops it. Because it's in society, making it politico-social, not a one-off charity, which devils in rock music to make its mark.

The war in colonialism embittered the island of Sri Lanka and the colour brown. The red Indians lost their way, but South Asia held firm. It wasn't a coincidence that Gandhi led the way of selflessness, which is our break. It must be. Not only, if you can be selfless anyway. But it captures the essence, and can help others along the way. Without worry.

The JVP stick to a Marxist agenda, which isn't bad. But doesn't lassoo the whole of the Colour. Brown I mean. Which it must, to be successful!! For the whole of the Colour. Brown I mean. Which it must, to be successful!! The Four countries that replicate it are India, Bangladesh, Sri Lanka and Pakistan, but all need to be in, regardless of religion and race, to make it work. Honestly!

The charity sectors works off donations and Buddhist or other religious shrines can't backfire without loss, so need the capitalist system in. So there's the conundrum. How do we get it, to You-Value, all the way through, however far off, and not in competition with Marxism or capitalism?

The You-Valuist agenda hasn't begun, but it can do, with perfection, if you keep it a try. No one needs to be selfless every day, at first, ongoing, but it is the colour atrue religious-wise, so make it slim, unconfrontational and happy, the Buddhist way, which is a hypothetical Buddhaland, which emphasises it most, I see, for all the four countries that make South Asia brown. Even

Hinduism has selflessness as its goal and Islam isn't devoid of it. So let's serve. Is generosity or service the goal? Gandhi said service. But Buddhists rook through happily to make the generosity aspect of capitalism a virtue too.

Even the west have aspects of You-Valuism through, like the council, which provide services for free, to tenants in council housing, so South Asia should too, with selflessness as its pride with no offence to oriental or white, or even black, who can all be selfless, and have proved it, with time, to make an altogether healthier lifestyle and atmos, which corresponds to an Earthly selflessness, only politically You-Valuist in scope.

This is the essence: A You-Value system that reaps the reward of selflessness, which is only just begun of late as an idea, historically, but doesn't exist in practise, full-blown, which it should do, well could do, and must, eventually, until it hurts not to partake in selfless acts daily, which is an all go to You, after a Me and then Us. A must. So let's keep slim. All is on the horizon. So let's get through, without trouble or hardship or animosity, because religions can keep, it's only the political situation that must change, and society. And colour brown gets us there, perhaps, because it already is selfless in scope religiously, one up from the cooperative "us" in Marx.

So don't worry. Don't' despair. Let's stay on, an earth ride that gets ungrim, and slowly help those beneath us, and let capitalism develop gradually, because society can even change first, until global, then the political and business realities will change automatically, with compassion, and ungrump, so lets dissolve in to a You-Value mode without changing our self to unstrong, so an individual essence can keep, without unkindly. Let's be, with or without You-Valuism in all the way through.

A Beautiful Mind, the well-acclaimed film, about John Knox, the famous mathematician, held a scene revealing Adam Smith, western philosopher, was wrong in making everything right on a competitive buzz, people acting selfishly, in own self-interest. So he devised a theory professing that if you act in the group as well as on your own, a better result produces.

You-Valuism, my theory, says, if you act in the interest of others, and so does everyone else, then the greatest wealth is generated. This You-Value drive deserves an unusual warrant for not being true, if others don't comprehend and act selfishly, then none of this is deserved. But if they, can, and will, or must will, this, true, then all is an unblemish, because it can win. Selflessness all-round is the timely even goal, until all is at rest and unsad, so people can live freely without fear or worry, and/or can carry selflessness without fear of attack. Even speedier, in lifestyle, it's a no worry if we win.

Not only wealth is the goal. Capitalism hopes to have a win-win game in place, but a you-value system depicts a society no longer at war, which capitalism failed to comprehend, so internal conflict can stop also. Let's be, again, and see if all works out, unselfishly, for an altogether brighter future, all the way to a You-value driveway to happiness on Earth right through upper and sturdier so all can warrant a right in to selflessly without fear either or each way, all-round and smartly.

Benjamin De Silva

A tri-polar world!

Not so long ago, when China visited Russia, one of the most common bonds the two nations expressed was a shared vision of a bi-polar world. There is capitalism and communism, but there can also be a third force – in South Asia, I say, which cherishes its own religious heritage - without extremism.

As I write, a new study was being prepared in California on the idea of Rebirth, or an afterlife, by Professor John Martin Fischer, an expert of philosophy, who is the project leader. He has been given millions of dollars to study the phenomena – and Eternalism!

But the idea of Rebirth is a quintessentially South Asian idea – at root, an idea that has huge ramifications for war and moral conduct generally, something that South Asia should be proud of, to say the least.

But you don't need to believe in Rebirth, to go beyond capitalism and communism. For, one can engage in spiritual conduct, selflessly, as well as politically, regardless, and work together on common themes without any blame, an idea expressed here, again, as You-Valuism, a step beyond both capitalism and communism. A You-Value polity, not just society, is what is meant, even if society can bring it in.

The fault, I think, with both capitalist and communist forms of governance is the emphasis is on goods, not people, on costs, not happiness.

At present, South Asia is in a transitory stage, as it will be - always. These are forever changing realms, this planet earth that we experience daily.

Just recently, Sri Lankan President Mahinda Rajapaksa had criticised the US-sponsored UNHRC resolution against his country and said the such "attacks would not defeat or intimidate us".

"This attack would not surprise us at all. These attacks would not subdue us either, nor would they defeat or intimidate us in any way", Rajapaksa said in the northwestern provincial district Kurunegala's military headquarters.

The President said he was better expecting such attacks from the pro-LTTE diaspora and anti-Sri Lanka elements when he was leading his army to militarily crush the LTTE's separatist campaign.

He also termed all allegations against his government as "false accusations with ulterior motives".

Alongside this, in South Asia, The Pakistan Taliban, a long while back, now, reportedly threatened to assassinate former military ruler Pervez Musharraf even as he had been granted pre-arrest bail by a Pakistani court.

Issuing a clear warning, Tehrik-e-Taliban Pakistan (TTP) spokesman IhsanullahIhsan said Musharraf will be the "main target" of the militants on his return. Ihsan asked Musharraf to surrender to the Taliban. In a video released, Saturday, the TTP had threatened that if Musharraf comes back to Pakistan then their suicide bombers and snipers will send him to "hell", as per reports.

In the six-minute video, both Ihsan and Adnan Rashid referred to the 2007 military raid on the radical Lal Masjid in Islamabad and said, "We will not leave you alive."

In Nepal, meanwhile, a United Nations Asia-Pacific regional seminar on human rights, sexual orientation and gender identity had, back then, called for the need for better laws to curb homophobic violence and discrimination in the society.

Inaugurating the two-day seminar, Nepalese Minister for Women, Children and Social Welfare Riddhi Baba Pradhan emphasised the need for legal, institutional and policy reforms in Nepal and elsewhere in taking the LGBTI (Lesbian, Gay, Bio-sex, Trans-gender and Intersex) movement forward.

The prevalence and gravity of homophobic violence and discrimination in the society is alarming, human rights officer, UN Headquarters Nikolaus Schultz said. "We should all be outraged when members of our human family are verbally abused, physically assaulted, arrested and sometimes killed simply because of whom they love or how they look," he said.

All these cases, decipher the need for a more spiritual approach to resolving strife in the region and afar – and the phenomena of Rebirth is a help even if not a prerequisite. Spiritual politics – or You-Valuism – would help make a tri-polar world, beyond capitalism and communism, at least at start, unless other regions follow suit, a much needed reality, and South Asia is good place to start because it already has a selfless polity potency.

Benjamin De Silva

The Selfless Gene: The Political Gap of the 2014 Elections

It is hard to imagine that a party cherishing *selflessness* could have made huge political gains in the 2014 local and European elections. And that's not what happened either. But, what if it were to emerge, some time, in the future? Would there be scope for a new political voice to fill the political vacuum of capitalism and socialist-leaning politics in the UK, not forgetting the one-issue parties like UKIP which say independence from Europe is what it's all about.

A new politically dynamic force, with mainstream appeal, compassionate and strong, has been off the cards for over a century, with the same old ideologies taking centre stage: Liberalism, Conservatism, Fascism, Socialism, Marxism and not much more, to adorn, or, more likely, moan about grimly. But the point about selflessness, is that it is a logical step up from Socialism, but hitherto unheard of in political debate or spin – deep-rooted philosophically!

So where did the idea spring from? It occurred to me, one day, when daydreaming, though in a more intuitive mode, that the selfish gene theory in science, which fears interplanetary colonisation, at some future date, is peculiar to the capitalist stage of societal functioning, where profit, greed and fear dominate the world scene untriumphantly. This I call the "Me-Value" society - and polity - where capitalist indicators mark the cornerstone of all policy, like the Socialists play with the mixed economy, not fully socialist yet, unfortunately, perhaps.

When we slip into war, world or more minor, territorially, this is a transgression to a "No-Value" let's say polity, to keep within the realm of political science, my field of focus, most importantly, to make the case for a selfless politics later on, more triumphantly this time. Maybe, society isn't ready for a true socialistic vision, despite the Labour advantage at the polls recently – the next stage in our political hierarchy, the "Us-Value" polity, because "Us" is for cooperation, but has the cooperative gene multiplied sufficiently to warrant a new form of politics? Still, Labour is spear-heading that genetic drive, unconsciously, yes, but surely, if even distribution of wealth was a socialist idea, one that meant, intrinsically, a more cooperatively-filled world.

Labour, in Britain, has, we all know, not only suffered serious debacles with the rise, then, of the SDP and what not, intermittently, but it has also won remarkably the support of society, with landslide prominence, on some occasions, in recent history, most glimmeringly, with the rule of Tony Blair, a political PR genius, who took his opponents to the doldrums with one success after another.

So it is this "No-Value" to "Me-Value" to "US-Value" transition which is at issue, because when society becomes more cooperative-driven, that will be Labour's heyday, and the ghost of capitalist expropriation will subdue ungracefully into the abyss of history, and socialism will make its mark, I hope, worldwide, some day. But there is another "gene" the scientists have left out, and that is the selfless gene, which most religions advance, admittedly sometimes hypocritically, but not undeservedly or un-needy.

The selfless gene, when it materialises in society, can give rise to what I call the "You-Value" polity, because it is selflessness towards the other, so we see, here, there is a definite progression of polities as: 'no', 'me', 'us' then 'you'; which takes us all the way to the vision of the enlightened few, like Buddha and Gandhi, but it is not as distant as might first seem, is it? So this is the *path*, up to a You-Value political system, however the *goal* is a selfless world, and the service sectors like Education and Health as well as charities epitomise what it means, ideally, and in practise, if will and ideals permit, to be selfless. Can we truly have a service-led society and economy, even in what is now the manufacturing sector, one day? Yes, this is what a You-Value polity – You-Valuism – means emphatically.

This is what the gap in the current political jungle is. It is the highest pinnacle of the political system unforeseen in ideological convictions and manifestos, but can wield leverage if harnessed correctly, and with enough foresight, innovation and mass appeal, in a way that transcends the socialist visions within the political landscape, abundantly. And that is what it should create – abundance. This space has yet to be capitalised on, but it exists. And only a highly compassionate leadership can bring it in.

Which new party in Britain next?

Lord Ashdown said, way back now, that plots to remove Nick Clegg, as party leader, should be "stopped now", but, the question of whether a, similarly, new party, more ambitiously-inclined than the Liberal Democrats, can be destined to take the moral high-ground, popularly, is more demanding than ever.

Not publicly, but in theory. Mainly, because it is not certain that socialism, in Labour's guise, is the highest stage of the political process, even as right-wing elements claim to have an, abundantly, higher moralising positioning, than Labour, especially, when it comes to business freedom, and other tenets.

Not even the far-left, have had their moral heyday, yet - god knows if they ought to, but could a new party in Britain, which is superior in ethical stance to Labour, at its best, make its way into British political life, despite this, and fend off the corresponding decay, that has stifled Britain for decades?

Indeed, displaying a morally-advanced status, without dither, may not be enough to warrant, handsomely, a successful, now desperately needed, propulsion, into a new kind of politics - selfless at core, and must go, if it is to thrive, in parallel with economic wisdom, and could, if capitalised on stringently, deliver the just society we've all idealised, but never fully realised, before.

Maybe, progressive elements in Labour, now unknown, could take the lead in this respect, and mould, decisively, a new political force which doesn't split the party, but moves it on, testing its ability to adapt to higher-than-socialist principles, than co-operation, perhaps, without losing the economic pragmatism, or earnest attempt at it, that its worked hard to build during the second-to-last Blairite-administration.

The grating suspicion of the Cold-War days has declined markedly, but China remains pioneering in its foreign policy. Still, a tri-polar world - with a new selfless party in place - heralding its own characteristics and preferences, the higher end of the political spectrum left-wise, need not be so uncanny, if the idea that socialism is politics' pinnacle is to be over-rid. And it can be.

The rewards of a selfless politics - upstaging socialistic values and profiteering capitalism -need not be a distant dream, provided the essence, unwaveringly, of this newer political offspring remains crystal clear and highly-focussed - with polices to match. After all, the encouragement of a selflessly-inclined world brings with it a return, by nature, of an all-receive-all climate - which must be good for everyone!

If some Labour MPs, at least, could bring You-Valuism – the theory of the selflessness of the polity – to the negotiating table, then a new chapter could dawn in the nature of politics, globally, eventually, where a world military is encouraged; where Social Mass Energy triumphs (n.b. you have to do good socially to see it not just expect it); where the end of suffering in the mind is adorned, and, where self-understanding is widely practised - making an altogether more self-conscious world.

The universe appears to have begun, miraculously or not, with negative energy, as epitomised in selfish gene theorising by proponents in science, but it is moving, with rapid-fire, towards higher life energies of compassion, tolerance and love. Bearing this in mind, the new politics proposed here, is not unmatchy with this version of events, but, instead, holds it up high cherishingly - and with unshakable optimism.

Given Britain's charitable and generous nature, too, it, the country, has the unquestionable potency to become the first You-Valuist state in history. Whether or not the genuine socialist movement in the UK was hijacked or not, for its part, still, with the essences of the political parties clearly lined-up for everyone to eye, abundantly, now, with mass media, it is unlikely, in all probability, that the general public could be hoodwinked if a new political party emerged that took selflessness as its central ideological positioning or heartfelt agenda.

Britain's next, new, political party should be of this kind, a force which takes politics into unchartered territory, boldly and enigmatically. Market analysis and ethics, are often far apart in the boardrooms, but a new type of moral marketing could help a new era of original and impactful policies reach the masses, both hearingly and emphatically.

Benjamin De Silva

Peace beyond Ukraine!

Russia's skirmishes with Ukraine are ambivalent and hypocritical. For, just as Russia lambasted Chechnya for its separatist intentions, all along, it later held close the pro-Russian separatists in Ukraine with a warmer heart. This is to be expected in a post-Soviet region which saw institutionalised Communism as the way, rather than, more stringently, a change in character towards a more cooperative mind-frame in persons, at least eventually.

Moscow's intolerance of religion and free speech, under the USSR, antagonised the pro-liberal forces that wanted to see reform, and jail terms of punk band Pussy Riot in Russia thereafter, still scent, of the freedom of expression momentum that underlined that cause, hand in hand with capitalism, as it was then and still is, largely.

Expectedly, religion has now resurfaced with tremendous grace and flamboyance in the newly formed independent states that made up the USSR. In the Guardian recently, a news item depicted the need to understand it, more specifically Christianity, rather than just act as church going faithists.

Separatism and religion remain two stumbling blocks of the modern era, where reconciling, separately, the two domains with society has collected numerous theories amongst various commentators and spokespeople, often at odds and counterproductive to consensus on the global political map.

Leftists have often scorned at religion, in traditional unguise. But character analysis reveals it is higher, morally, on the virtue apparatus, than many of its preceding antidotes like Capitalism, and indeed, Socialism.

The true progress path to a higher value world is the following: profit, cooperation, selflessness.

The Ukraine dilemma, sits awkwardly in a democracy-related conundrum that tests whether people, in this day and age, are allowed, to choose their political destiny. And they should be able to. But this macro picture outlined above, is the driving force of political development, and neither Ukraine nor Russia should bow out of it, if real change in people's persona is ever going to steer upwards – religiously, even if not overtly.

People must transform - selflessly-bound - for real institutional reform to follow. And it can happen. The shift from feudal to capitalist society heralded, alongside The Enlightenment, a similar transformation. But, for higher moral progress, the succeeding chapters in human history must surface decisively.

World peace goes beyond the separatist issue. Religion has its part to play. That the Pope welcomed Middle Eastern heads of states to pray for peace, is the correct mode of play for religious leaders in the current climate of fear and hostility in war-hit areas of conflict. But more needs to be done, to harness virtuous action in common daily life until it spreads throughout society.

If world socialism hasn't materialised yet, it is because the cooperative mind-set hasn't been firmly established in society world-wide before the money-motivated inclination of all business endeavours. But to go beyond cooperation, is another thing entirely. As of yet, no polity higher than socialism has been envisaged until now. And that's when selflessness all-round takes over.

Benjamin De Silva

Buddha's Vision

That life can go on? Or was it just the end of suffering? Or both? Let's say the middle pick. So how do we get there, so You-Value politics can fit? We say, get on the Zero train, the evolve of the mind to a Zero peace of emptiness, after binary good/bad or just good next, let's say.

This is Zero Psychology, if the experts want to follow the Buddha's path!! So let's brim in, to no froth and let the Zero games begin. All is a one-wash, if all comply, because united we stand, united we win!

So go on, be careful, because Mindfulness means this, but you start with awareness, a true understanding of reality as it is, as you go on unsternly but gentle, if you can, cos we all need some less trouble and it is if we keep underestimating ourselves without wobble.

This is the space of Zero, pure awareness, where we can see and act accordingly, so a response, not an act, unharshly but not unbrimmed. All is not lost with Zero Psychology, because we can evolve or develop more nicely if we encounter a lot of sternness, over the pitch!!

Footballers can be nice and their enthusiasm glow, but more mindful, without worry, means it can last. Don't succumb either, cos all is not lost, with the action near, even the cops can have a go, and unsuspect wrong trouble, even if it has to be near.

But let's not go too far. Some times the police have to arrest, when investigation leads it to an ill will, because that's what The Buddha did, he arrested suffering, saying there was a way out, and there is, but it has to be all round and global, even earthly.

Don't rest assured, be on the go, cos that's how to investigate, everything you come across, not unlike the police, but better, cos you can see what people think from the Zero spot, where emptiness and peace collide, and from here, everything makes sense, even your day to day dealings. No police trouble. All is on, for everyone, if they can see, unblindly, and self-arrest, when the suffering increases, which it will, if you don't take care.

So this is it. The end of suffering and Deathless on, Buddha's vision for man, or mankind, and it must work, if we all agree to a you-value polity to go along with it. Let's not cause trouble, because it will rebound with Karma and Rebirth in, if it is. Paranoid schizophrenia and other mental illnesses may be wrong for others, but sometimes it is right. Even depression, some say, has to exist, if external vehicles block or ungrope you with added vigour, so you feel restless and hopeless. Externally created mental illness by others is the wash. So keep clean.

So, let's let it in, until we can whither away the mental health institutions, when everyone is on a Zero skill game, always, and without bother. Let's hope it wins, because Buddha meant it, and people led the way. Now we have a fifth of the global population near it, and it can win. Let's not cause any bother, and make Zero psychology win!!!

How Christianity Groaped The 'You'!

Selflessness isn't the abode of just South Asia. The capitalist-break-away bunch and the Christian unscrum, make individual persona break the mould, and can also do so by making selflessness and everlasting life the ungrey which takes us back to the heyday of Adam and Eve and the luxurious garden, which Earth can be. As did the Catholics and other non-Eastern religions. Giving more than you receive and loving oneself and God, makes selflessness outside and within the reason to be, a you-value grace which makes everyone peak, not just trough. So let's begin, or did it, the world, so who created, was it just a whim and why should we win?

Yes, the world could have been created by a loving father, but who's to say he didn't return to live in it, this Earth, and why can't more than one person have collaborated to make it a success? So, how did it start, this universe and Earth pit? Let's see.

Was it an Adam and Eve's heavenly scent before we got worse, or did we start with bacterial life like the scientists implicit? Either way, we can get to a Heaven, one assumes, not sure, if we follow the Buddha's path of removing all suffering and mental anguish, as the start, to make it a 'you' instead of 'no', 'me, or just 'us' as the communists do.

Yes, the heavenly non-religious types can win, too. Not always, but even atheists can see materially that we can create a heaven, and we should do. Let's not be unsure. Because we need certainty and Buddhists and other religions follow suit, not unwholeheartedly, but the correct way, which is a must.

All religions suffice. Not just Buddhism or Hinduism, nor Islam, but the western and African religions, if they pave the way for selflessness and non-disgrace. We are on a road to non-hell, so we can win, if we keep the pace and let others follow suit.

Christianity tops the board, by making religion in a non, no a pro-capitalist world, the top priority, we hope, so that peace can ensure victory for all, and so the Deathless, or everlasting life, can triumph, and, ideally, so that we have legislation in place to avoid murders and make it happen one day while in, the sooner the better, if it can.

So who's to stop it, if eternity and immortality can add on life hope, not take it away, until it is not non-graced but paternally kind and familiar to all, for all, and everyone? So be prepared for the eternal light, if it comes, again, one day, for all to see, because Earth deserves it, and it can meet!!

Religion is the pathway to the 'You' in us all, where You-Valuism becomes the polity and selflessness is encouraged in us all, until it doesn't matter what you do, or whatever win you have, because no one cares for jealousy since all is on an 'all get all' if it can ever happen, which it must.

Let's hope we get there, so all can win!! – even religions!

Are planned external causes of mental
illness much more frequent than inner turmoil?

The Mirror newspaper, revealed, just recently, that child abuse of kids in mental health wards was a top issue, without worrying the establishment. Or was it, like this? No, not really. Just after a parliamentary watchdog said it will look into the issue, we uncovered more.

The idea that we are mentally ill parse, has been exposed as false! We are just ill. But what is less cared for is that outside causes could be the reason, not internal worry - primarily. Or no? with or without internal worry is the issue, or, in some cases, both.

One medicinal expert has warned, using Buddhist philosophy that a name has been given to this externally caused phenomena in ancient literature. "Supermundane", is the label given to it as external, and, internally, the branding, in scriptures, not the medicine Buddha – is, "mundane". Whether true or false, in terminology, which is it, for you?

That is the question. In one scenario, kept quiet for personal reasons, the family even set up incidences of hypnotic persona change to make a person look ill to avenge his death, by showing he was seeing people in odd situations as if bewildered by visual hallucinations, by acting an on spot culprit in chosen designations where the patient could see him, only later to reveal that it wasn't him, on several occasions. What a blunt stunt. The family later returned grace when they were later found out.

In one broadcast on mental illness using schizophrenia as its guise, by non-culprits, they successfully expose, in brand imaging, that it takes one to make physical illness, but two to make mental. The point is simple. Never let others control you by setting up situations where you are seen as the victim of mental health on your own, when actually they are conspiring to reduce it, your mental health, as a persona of corrupt investigation, when they were ill to begin with, perpetrated by it, as a condition, because of their own ill health, to do it in the first instance.

You-Valuism: The Scripture

The same goes for mental institutions. Who's to say the treaters are not mentally ill with the same disposition in mental clinics and hospitals? Our study shows that the vast majority of the world is culminating to a service kind of mentality, even within families, but only in a capitalist framework, and that man hasn't evolved, yet, much far, for most, beyond this point. The implication is astonishing: That we are living in a world of greed, starvation and hopelessness, for many, where even service suffers as a result!!

This means, that we are starting off from a point of selfishness classified as a 'me' value society and business framework, where mental health is at the crux of our distaste for things obviously not given in a state of free, or, good, will. Which it must be, if we are to survive. The Communists say that cooperation is the next step in our value structure, so an 'us' value system is required to build character on. The last step, is a 'you'.

South Asia, in brown skin colour, is a selfless abode which characterises the 'you-value' system in evolutionary thought, the most, which our new book, entitled, in part, You-Valuism, now published, here, warrants. Because it is a 'stop'! We have to unslumber and awake, so we can be more untroubled by the world we live in. If externally caused mental illness is the key, then the perpetrators are themselves mentally ill and disturbed – and we need to achieve a 'you-value' development of moral progress, to allow service to be what it is.

Self-Realisation or Self-Understanding!!

By now, it should be apparent that Self-Realisation is on the verge of collapse, with less than selfless personas roaming, even under-transforming their lives away by picking fights that should be left to the cauldron.

It is a common theme in Hinduism, Buddhism and Vedic theory, which is individual-to-social in nature, and claims to know our persona, with some, even on the go, especially in higher reaches of religion. But it is vital to know where we are, to find out where we have to be, and get there to avoid the wrath of Karma and Rebirth without too much harshness in our spirit, now uplifted when we find out who we are.

People have many mind-made powers in society, and it is taught in guru-led Indian society, but where will this get to, especially the power of self-transformation in physical experience, which we've witnessed totally, even if it's used, in film, as an antagonistic guise, unproudly, though some use it, there, and now, to protect, if you can?

But how can a mind infested with hate and impurity make you win, if it is on a spy-type mentality, like some, that tries to deceive and get away with things to take off others who are morally superior if all that we wish for isn't pure or puritanical in non-guise, which it should be?

Self-realisation is the art of knowing who you are, however harsh, until it bleeds goodness and calm for knowing where you fit into the picture of life, so you can surround yourself with the best pick, and make right choices.

So let's do it, however humble we have to be in the process!!

So where do we go from here on?

The way of Self-Realisation is to find ways of being yourself, without harking on about material position and who likes you or not, however clever/unclever it might be to try. We have to witness ourselves and find out from the mind who we happen to be – even Godly!

From thereon in, we can be true to you and make ends meet in a happier less unfree manner until we can envelop a new way of being that is test-worthy and apparent to all, if it links us to our true being.

So, this is how to progress, with Self-Realisation! We have to know where to begin, and, according to all eastern tradition, including Tao, it is with ourselves, who we are, and how we happen to respond to circumstances, which we can change, if inferior, slowly and step by step!!

So let's unturnip, and make a start. Know who you are, and be better. Progress gradually, and take a new insight of yourself each day, until all is selfless and calm, without looking over your shoulder to see who can see.

They are only gripe, and in this dangerous world, with Karma, and we suspect, Rebirth, in, no one gets away with anything. Yes, Self-Realisation is the start, but we can proceed and develop, which we must. So, eventually we will win, and get to the selfless spot where You-Valuism, the persona of selflessness, begins.

Benjamin De Silva

NON-SUPERIORITY!!

The you-value structure outlined doesn't mean a superior trend in polity. It is just 'what could be', not 'what is', but where we want to go. It's selflessness, not non-attachment or Nirvana, in Buddhism, according to political life, but a step up from co-operation as an 'us' value stream!!

Let's not defend. All is on the up, or could be, if we comprehend that all is a value, again, stream in political, not to mention, business life. So we shall see. Gramsci invented 'Hegemony' to reflect the domination of cultures. Well here, we're talking about the value indices, which take us on higher, to a far off place where we all want to dig our heels in.

So let's comprehend, instead of unvigour, that all in life is moving towards an end that is selflessly free, where all is in the heat of tropical nurturing of moral, again, heat, so one can be clean of any decimation of thirst for greed, and one can envisage a future where all is free and true, and people live in harmony and grace, until all is neat and saffron, unrobey!

Let's leave it there, until we see that superiority in political system is a strife that no one should contend with, because all is the same until we differ, and people on the path there should be helped, not harmed, as Ajahn Sumedho, now well known, in Buddhism, told us frequently in this life episode.

So let's make it work and prepare for the best, including the US, where Stoicism is already beginning to hold, the idea that military should not ruin itself in its grief but deliver according it more happily for all is not lost if we compliment the ancient non-antagonisers in the political rim, where no one is superior or inferior unless you take moral toll and lose as a result by keeping unclean.

So lets win, now, and non-surrender for the evolution up to a You-value spirit!

Selflessness in small doses

No one is saying a You-value spirit of selflessness need be a big pick up, for now, only small doses is what the Buddha said to be happy, like a drip drip of water pouring, no tipping into a mug is how happiness grows.

And the same goes for the political structuring and the executive in policy terms. We don't have to howl or seek revolutionary solutions, only calm getaways that can help even the smallest child with a lost bus ticket provided by an authority if she gets lost going to school.

Don't wait. You-Valuism needn't be in to start. Small acts of selflessness by the polity like this is where to begin until all is on a selfless split. So don't' frown. It's easy as piss. The dole queue is one example, but why ought it be ruthless, and worth disability benefit. Why can't we just stay, until all is ripe without worry of the authorities taking us away?

But there is no excuse in South Asia, especially brown skin type, where most of the You-value religions first originated. There, there need not be any worry of giving kindly to people in need. And there shouldn't be.

The same applies to Europe and Africa, where we need to begin a selfless spirit, not just working out cost as in the capitalist system, so You-value all the way. The problem with communist explosions is too much was done on the structural level, but not enough on the societal/personal level where true co-operation, not to mention love, begins. So, we can't leave it all up the polity. Selflessness begins at home. So let's leave it there and hope no one moans.

The greatest threat to a You-Valuism of this kind is that we want it all at once. It's a gradual process just like our Buddha. So let it spread. At home first, then in the jungle. Don't be alarmed if all is not as one, initially. But it will be. Keep going and let's never give in.

The so-called "third world" now, with you-Valuism, in the polity, exposed as a myth, hasn't done enough, to build a more caring world where even the west has taken the lead before it, despite being more advanced spiritually - for lack of money.

But that problem needs to be overcome if South Asia brown is to realign and take its rightful place on the leadership stage where it belongs at near the pinnacle, where it must be. Until now, with colonialism, the capitalist history has come to the fore in our countries, which is wrong, ideally, and spiritually.

Well now it can change. No one needs to be first, only right. And You-Valuism is the right political system for South Asia eventually if the social realities there are to be taken into account as a selfless spirit, in ideal. So the communal and colonial shackles can be took off, and a new modern era begun. Let's see and hope it manifests, wisely and in time, because South Asia deserves a highly modern dole queue just as much as the west and needs to find the money to make it rest easily therein for a start.

GLOBALISATION IN KARMALAND!!! NOW HOLD STRONG

China has punished almost 20,000 officials in the last year, former reports say, for breaching rules to cut down on bureaucracy as well as pomp and ceremony, according to the government and Yahoo strong.

President Xi Jinping had ordered the crackdown, unsmiley, then late last year, he said, when he became head of the ruling Communist Party, seeking to take out public anger at waste and extravagance, particularly officials seen abusing their position to illegally amass wealth.

So where has it all gone?

Xi demanded meetings be shortened, over-the-top welcoming ceremonies ditched, and wordy, meaningless speeches abandoned, as he sought to cut red tape and make the country's bureaucracy more efficient and less prone to graft.

So where does true Co-operation come, not spring, from, atrue – Unmarxisty? From sharing of course!! So is this a new form of Globalisation? Of course not, just less evangelical. So, when are the conditions right, for less Competition whither? That's the unanswered question. And that's the West's way with Marxy proper, not to overtake!! So that's a conditional analysis, in Marxism, afresh today, now. Not a You-value one, less competitive, and sturdy, if run first from, in South Asia, timely and truth-wise.

So, in academia, is Globalisation new? In context it is, but not in idea! Marxism has it!!

In actual terms, it's saying when the conditions are fresh, new developments can alter, like food delivery across borders - but nothing stupid! Which is 'dependent origination!' in Buddhism, only applied to the real world, not to the Earth, but world, where humans live, not apes or monkeys, nor sea world either. Or wind, whatever, Oh! God, lives in there!!

So, that's the real perspective! The idea that when the conditions are there, things, or whatever, arise! And that's it, every inch, not bit, of the World-Earth-Map, now, which can calm on, to a higher morality, if true.

So, what is Globalisation in these historic definitional terms, to see if I alter?

Is it, as one Buddhist title explains,: "…, embedded in the cardinal doctrine of interdependence or dependent co-arising, also translated as dependent co-origination, conditioned genesis, or conditioned co-production?!" Yes, the same.

Another definition.".the process by which businesses or other organizations develop international influence or start operating on an international scale." [Similar interpretation to some acclaimed journalists. So, can be, like Dependent Origination, even mildly, or better than previously explained in similar titles, not without unknowns in.

Wikipedia says Globalisation is! "the process of international integration arising from the interchange of 'world views' products, ideas, and other aspects of culture'. Advances in 'transportation' and 'telecommunications', infrastructure, including the rise of the 'telegraph' and its posterity the 'Internet', generating further "interdependence" of economic and cultural activities. Similar to type 1.

So how is it so true to what I've described earlarly?

The Business Dictionary, online, implicits, no it is, not unsurely, that Globalisation, is the worldwide movement toward economic, financial, trade and communications integration.

It blossoms that! Globalization implies the opening of local and nationalistic perspectives to a broader outlook of an interconnected and interdependent world with free transfer of capital, goods, and services across national frontiers.

However, it envisages…, it does not include unhindered movement of labour [even transformerly] and, as suggested by some economists, may hurt smaller or fragile economies if applied indiscriminately. That should hold, though there are other, less fragile, definitions.

Let's stay with number 1, which is closer, but not entirely, now, to Dependent Origination, precise, and implicitly!

You're not alone with Karma in, either, you're near! Yeah, that's right!!

Let's unexplain the origins of the universe, and make it a reality that wins, not impolitely, not has to be, alright, if all can be all-right here on Earth, in essence, not just globally, or impeccably, but perfectly, if it is, not the way it is, if one can decipher the meaning of it.

That explains it, Globalisation, I sure, however non-unkindly, because kindness is the key, an open key to You-Valuism, when the conditions are there, not a has to be, until all becomes certain from uncertain, all the way through. However tight! Or boring. That will do. Yeah, let's leave it there generously true, not bloody tight! Yeah, let's look through, or view higher. Sorry for the over snob!! That's globalisation in a nutshell!!

Benjamin De Silva

So who are the true Philosopher Kings of Plato?

(A self-appraisal)

Plato, the western philosopher, said that the rulers of any state should be experts in philosophy. But are they – experts – in politics, really?
Are political philosophers good, either? They should be, or politics can't blend with religion, eventually, where it should, on virtue, especially selflessness, close to the South Asian community, powerful, and in every South Asian-based religion there, not now, but in the future.

So how should they get there? Seeming Divine Eye or Divine Ideation experiments, by Benjamin De Silva, say that people here on Earth have a "flame or fame?" philosophy originally, after man evolved, co-ordinated by the first global Buddha in history.

He, I see, saw that man sought, ideally, notoriety for inhuman action, like murder, which the police are up against, brought about by shameful defeat in war, so he advised that seeking notoriety, again, for good things, like music and achievement was best for them. Hence the evolution of fame.

ISHI, me, former Asian Times Editor (UK), said: "The need for a more expansive philosophy, which exists now, more friendly, should be cultivated, beyond pleasure even, in these trying times like Utilitarianism was!!!"

"Surely people are more wise now, and can go beyond just this ego driven attitude reminiscent in some. Notoriety for good beyond fame is pleasant and needs to be digested with something less horrid. Man has evolved far now to capitalism, and the next stage is due – world-wide"
"Political philosophers should now, the time is right, to set an example, and proceed into politics wisely and with Socialism and

You-Valuism in mind. They can do it, rather than capitalists. They should set the example".

So, should political philosophers quit? No. Because the next stage in history must be "Socialism as the politics of cooperation". So they must get there, into power, not like in Sri Lanka where even Buddhist monks have a try, where they shouldn't.

Meditations say Buddhism is a response to racists abroad using a strategy of suicide against the Sri Lankan populace, the reason Buddhism survived in Sri Lanka and not other South Asian countries, especially.

Hence, the end of existence thesis in the religion. So why try killing yourself, if there is an easy way in, not out? Because once started, the need to kill one-self vanishes because of all the generosity, kindness and love unburdened thereafter.

Socialism, with co-operative states globally, rather than capitalist, is also the way in, politically, but not without possibility. Former British Prime Minister, Edward Heath said "politics is the art of the possible", so we only gave the structure, not the outcome, but the risk is essential, risk everything to win the possibility of Socialism on a global scale for mankind and end world war, finally, where a higher fame, rather than flame the planet with an world-war inferno, wins, as well as, mild accomplishment true thereafter.

If the persona exists, now, with Socialism as a step up from "me" under capitalism to "us" under socialism, world-wide, then others, when in power, especially political philosophers, then, have the freedom to devise possibilities innovatively ongoing afterwards, in actual trade, and other, relations to end poverty and make things less brutally social, nice and happy. That's how, I think, they should go on!!

The game is for "The World Federation Of Socialist States" to end world war, before You-Valuism, without expansionism, colonisation and racism, which it can be when we envisage something higher and stick to it regardless of colour, creed or race, and work for each other's interests, not collectives but co-operative, especially in politics, since the economy can follow – later, not now.

The political philosophers, unlike Plato, have to get there, in power, smart and happy, so the real experts of politics, not philosophy, take the lead, gradually, but not unsurely – even with police monitoring – global.

ISHI took on the hope of establishing World Socialism, after regular encouragement by his father, as a child on up, to "change the world" for the betterment of mankind until everyone can live in a free, no poverty in, planet, for all.

South Asian leadership & spiritual politics in a capitalist world!

Can South Asia be a regional leader in the world despite the US seeing itself as the lead global player? What is South Asia's true place in the world, both politically and spiritually? Does the role of religion act as a catalyst for a world leadership role, or does it weaken the prospect of secular polities with less violence in the form of religious wars?

The truth is South Asia can be "big", despite the economic, not spiritual, poverty in most of its states, with the exception of India, if only the countries there see the relevance of *selfless* and/or *egoless* spirituality to politics.

The four ascending value-systems below say it all:

1. The Existential attitude of "Anything Goes"
2. The "Me" Value system of Capitalism
3. The   "Us"   Value   system   of Socialism/Communism
4. And the "You" Value moral systems of Buddhism, Hinduism, Islam, Christianity, Catholicism, Judaism etc.

South Asia falls, or can do, potentially, into this latter category – foremost!

This You-value system, the highest, here, in the scale, then, is what can distinguish South Asia from the rest of the world, and offer it hope, peace and, above all, leadership. In this sense, South Asia can be, and indeed is, well placed to be a, if not *the*, global leader. Indeed, this You-value positioning surpasses both the capitalist and socialist systems of governance as can be seen above.

The Gandhi-led Indian independence movement, of course non-violent, is evidence of this You-value system at work in South Asia, in particular, the inherent morality in his approach to liberation. It is the absence, however, of this You-value stance that has led to the often violent and authoritarian, not to mention brutal episodes of conflict in the region afterwards.

Self-awareness, in South Asia, of what the region and its people *ought* to represent is what is needed. It is a step even beyond Socialism, which Karl Marx so readily recommended as the solution to all the ills of capitalism. The point is, because religion is so dominant in the region, the morality and spirituality of it needs to be harnessed for the benefit of people wider than religion.

If this can be done, South Asia, could be a real global leader, rather than trying to compete with the West in economic terms and the rest of it, pursuits of a Me-value variety kind in our breakdown. On the contrary, South Asia does have a role to play in the world, and naturally leans, in terms of its people, to this You-value spirituality, as the strength of religion in this region clearly demonstrates.

This is not to mix up religious fundamentalism with true, You-value moral ethics, but only to show that You-value spirituality like compassion and altruistic love are a *progression,* logically, from Existentialism, Capitalism and Socialism/Communism, whether we like it or not.

States should provide the means whereby people can exercise this compassion, even if it means endorsing, one day, even if not now, a *world* socialist system as the next step in the development of human societies, as a start, but not necessarily as a final vision.

But it should not be done at the expense of religion!

People, not states, religion or money, are the problem. Since, religions and states are composed of people, and those pursuing profit are people too, motivated by various intentions. So, this is where spirituality comes in. For this reason, *South Asian states should take the lead in building a spiritual world, something which is beyond both capitalism and communism.* This is South Asia's unique, in-built potential, which is at the highest end of the value system scale, for all societies, even higher than socialism, as we have seen above.

To this end, South Asia leads, or, more precisely, *can* lead, even The United States of America, and not to mention mankind as a whole, by becoming the first global region to *ethically* transcend both capitalism and communism – one day, however far off. Indeed, that would make South Asia true leaders in what otherwise amounts to a haphazardly unpredictable capitalist world.

South Asia's 'Non-Aligned Movement' during the Cold War where it sided with neither the Soviet Union, nor capitalist states such as the US, may have been a rather *wise* move in this regard, because it now allows South Asia, if the will exists, to pursue a more moral, and spiritual, politics, domestically and internationally, that is truer to its own religious heritage.

Benjamin De Silva

Reconciling Materialism & Idealism

The materialist/idealist debate in philosophy can be transcended if we see - both - mind and matter moving to the same end – the total elimination of suffering (Buddha's purpose for mind), and that would equal Heaven (Christianity, Catholicism, Judaism, Islam) but in this life not an afterlife, even if an afterlife exists.

Buddhism and Hinduism could also be incorporated into this model if the road to Heaven on Earth is seen to take place over life episodes, the concept of Rebirth, a kind of spiritual materialism. Karl Marx only said the first four stages of history (primitive man, feudalism, capitalism and then socialism/communism). But, could the next stages lead us all the way to Heaven, even if Earth is seen by scientists to have a limited timespan? And would this model be a good way of overcoming religious, scientific and philosophical differences – a Cern request?

Both Buddha and Hegel put an emphasis on Mind as primary while materialists like Marx, put matter first. Hegel was what is known as an "idealist" — according to him, mental things (ideas, concepts) are fundamental to the world, not matter. Material things are merely expressions of ideas — in particular, of an underlying "Universal Spirit" or "Absolute Idea."

Marx joined the "Young Hegelians" (with Bruno Bauer and others) who were not simply disciples, but also critics of Hegel. Although they agreed that the division between mind and matter was the fundamental philosophical issue, they argued that it was matter which was fundamental and that ideas were simply expressions of material necessity. This idea that what is fundamentally real about the world is not ideas and concepts but material forces is the basic anchor upon which all of Marx's later ideas depend.

Absolute idealism is Hegel's account of how existence is comprehensible as an all-inclusive whole. Hegel called his philosophy "absolute" idealism in contrast to the "subjective idealism" of Berkeley and the "transcendental idealism" of Kant and Fichte, which were not based on a critique of the finite and a dialectical philosophy of history as Hegel's idealism was. Here, the exercise of reason and intellect enables the philosopher to know ultimate historical reality, the phenomenological constitution of self-determination, the dialectical development of self-awareness and personality in the realm of History.

For his part, while the Buddha advised the people to take steps to alleviate poverty and establish a sound economic base, he constantly warned them about the dangers of falling victims to consumerism. The Buddha presented various precautionary measures to avoid falling into the clutches of consumerism which induces individuals not only to exploit his fellow beings but even the environment which is so vital for the survival of the humankind. He used an apt parable about a fig fruit glutton to show the danger as well as the folly of succumbing to consumerism. In the same source the Buddha advocates the practice of balanced life (Samajivikata) as an effective check against whole heartedly embracing consumerism.

Ajahn Jagaro, a modern day monk, states: "In Buddhism we say that we strive to protect ourselves and to protect others. By protecting myself, I protect others, by protecting others, I protect myself. So the aim of a Buddhist is to create outer harmony and inner peace. We say that "The mind is the forerunner to all things". The quality of the mind is that which determines the quality of life, so that if we see continuous strife, confusion and conflict in the world, wars, discriminations and exploitations then that can only reflect the quality of the minds of human beings. So the individual minds of human beings must also be in a state of confusion, conflict, oppression and aggression, because all actions, whether good or bad, have "mind as the forerunner". In Buddhism we place great emphasis on the mind. We train the mind so that we begin to understand the mind, and ultimately to liberate it."

But the resolution of the mind/matter dilemma, as expressed above, may be helped along by considering – both – mind and matter as important, and essentially having a dual purpose. If mind is moving to the end of suffering, in Buddhist eyes, then so, too, can material reality. Heaven may well be the end product of the development of human societies as scientific and technological advances make that prospect all the more plausible.

MASS ENERGY, with social in!

There's been a lot of talk about mass surveillance in the news recently. But "what if" the interconnection of senses opens it up thereafter. Or was it before? The social energy unleashed could be lethal. And it was. Even up to the media. But what's so astounding about turning the tables? Yes, by making Social Mass Energy (SME) a positive force in the world, says ISHI.

Even in individual components, as a sum total, SME is vital. So what is it? The premise: *You have to be good to see more good in the world, not just expect it!* Different from cooperation in Marxism. Or Karma in Buddhism, which is more individual. Though Buddhism and Karma can take a social form in other respects. Not often explained, but SME is derived from it! On an energy flow, though, the happier energy exchange emanating from combined mixing of positive actions atmospherically, and even in gain.

So how did SME come about in me, deeper? It's a product of Interconnectivity in Buddhism, but for a higher end. At present, all interaction, virtually, or considerably, on a social scale, is sour or getting that way. Charity is an exception. But the pinnacle of Interconnection at the highest, means all is a virtuous exchange. That's the start of Inter-being, or could be, a well-known concept in eastern tradition. To just be with what you adore, not run after it, haphazardly. However temporary or not it may be.

But we're miles away from it right now. But don't need to be. So, what would it bring? A host of natural pleasures, and happiness beyond belief, socially! But that's not the only point worth a try. SME is good in itself if it brings relief and joy. The down swing of what seems to us to be the senses, or inner intuition, which picks up prematurely, in society, sometimes uncontrollable, has been classed, in some literature, maybe unwarrantably, as a take of the "6 uncontrollables".

Others say, more notably, how the sense pick up a-bold, put down to the sixth sense of the mind, included in the six uncontrollables, which are eye, nose, touch, tongue, ear and mind, is only a happier if motivated by wholesome motivation. Otherwise it is classed as an illness. But SME correlates if even sense goes are guided by virtue, even of a pleasurable kind, not just happier, though pleasure without happiness is considered unkind, then all is not unkind.

In some philosophy, the infinite potential for good exists in a Zero slant, mind empty for rationality, not a sense one, as such, at least not all the way, without an experiential hover. This means the infinite mind can create untold opportunities for good. That's the evolve of the mind to an empty, beyond sense, intuitive mind-set, that is freer than the sense organs. Whether true or false, is less kindly than a try. But SME operated from this front, is kind, self and outer, say I.

The free mind has delivered the ultimate sense of knowledge say its authors, which is not happiness par se, but freedom-related, a delivery to freedom, a deliverance of mind that is a further enhancement of mind that is stronger afield than other manly powers, however tight the environment warrants. This 'may' be its start. SME gets us there. More freedom comes to those who are good. The more, the merrier.

Does the Universe have an objective purpose?

Yes. The Universe has a purpose. Karma and Rebirth are there to develop the mind or soul or heart, to qualify us for higher levels of existence, in other world systems, perhaps, and the world is like a school where we learn such things as compassion and universal love to get there.

This is the theory being proposed by one thinker, who preferred to stay anonymous, for now, a master of philosophy from Kings College, London, who challenges the view in Theravada Buddhism that it's all about ending Karma and Rebirth so that our lives therefore end in "nothing".

Instead, the Universe, Karma and Rebirth are there for a reason. It is not just the way it is. If we fall foul of Karma, we suffer in this life, and, perhaps, over Rebirths, but if we act in accordance with Karma, we flourish, far better, and move to higher realms – an infinite number.

It's all about developing the mind, the teleology (or purpose) - that Aristotle assigned to mother nature, saying that the physical manifestation of exterior existence is meaningful.

All of this makes life worth it!

Karma and Rebirth have an objective purpose: to develop the mind, precisely. In some realms, we could envisage the mind being superior to matter whereby mind can determine bodily existence, not succumb to death etc. Nor need all universes be temporary. The mind is on a journey. And this is just a single life episode designed to cultivate the mind in that direction.

It's not just a changing stream of consciousness that migrates, life after life, as in Buddhism, but a developing or potentially developing mind.

This is the purpose of the universe and existence, then!

So, does this hypothesis stand up?

According to Flora Graham, the digital Editor of the New Scientist, the prestigious scientific journal in the UK, there is no scientific proof for Rebirth and Karma. The scientific consensus, she says, at present, is, that the universe began with the Big Bang, and prior to that there was nothing. Nothing turned into something and nature is just developing according to certain laws.

Leaving aside the work of Dr Ian Stevenson, who tested child memories of kids who could remember past lives, Buddhism, too - in some quarters, says the universe started from nothing.

But if Karma and Rebirth do exist, then how could something so intricate have developed from mere nothing? Perhaps, the starting point was "potential energy", not just nothing. And from this, Karma and Rebirth emerged to develop mind into ever higher levels, with a DNA-like origin.

Paul Harris, Spiritual Director of the Aukana Trust, a UK Buddhist centre of the Theravada tradition, however, says that both Karma and Rebirth exist in the same way that the law of gravity exists; they are all part of nature. He adds that proof of their existence comes through mindful examination of one's own subjective experience. For instance, personal knowledge of which actions actually lead to pleasant results which means that you will be able to make intelligent choices about your behaviour and therefore enjoy far more happiness in your life.

He goes on, this does not mean that the laws of Karma and Rebirth have any inherent 'ultimate purpose' any more than gravity has an 'ultimate purpose'. For the Buddhist, life is an endless flow of conscious experience with no discernible beginning or end. True freedom is not a destination, rather it is simply understanding how life works born of careful observation of one's own experience.

So far, the question of whether existence has an objective purpose remains unresolved, as now does whether Karma and Rebirth reinforce this view. For now, the scientists have yet to fully explore the consequences of Karma and Rebirth theory, for understanding our world.

But if the ancient philosophers, like Plato and Aristotle, are right, then, perhaps, there is a reality beyond what we commonly experience as life, which is free from suffering and strife. And the purpose of life, aided by Karma and Rebirth, is to develop the mind in order to get there.

How to overcome poor looks!

A strange day arose when I was first accompanying journalism. I was invited to BBC World on a placement, which I took on earnestly. But, again, a peculiar thing happened. I began discussing problems in Sri Lanka, and there was a bit of a disagreement with the Editor.

I had asked the Editor there, why the media had crippled in failing to report the fate of Sri Lankan Tamils properly, despite opposite terror on each side and a government media ban there at the time, nor the later alleged need for war crimes investigations after the war, something I contend.

Better to reconcile and unify than waste time on the past. Thinking about the past, only leads to repeating history, as Ajahn Brahm, head monk of the Buddhist society of Western Australia, so succinctly points the way, without horror or unleashing criticism. Forgiveness, as always, is a much wiser weapon, untimely for some, but not departed in a You-Value environment where all is well, not only mentally but materially too. After all, you could give money for free if all is you-value by government not banks, if distribution and production is, likewise, offered, on a freely come freely go basis.

A good point, perhaps, not unkindly, for the "third world" to consider! To avoid monetary deficit. The problem, so far, has been, that the production wing doesn't give freely, only the money supply has been recommended. But this way, even goods and services such as building contraction for environment, are just given away with no need to rid ourselves of the monetary or financial system or supply, which would raise standards universally or globally, as all is selfless in productioning, giving way to internal development for one as key, let's say, at ideal pinnacle.

However, getting back to the mystery, when asking about the BBC's reluctance to get to the truth, and instead remain unwieldingly independent, a time-honoured framework, something uncanny came forth. Now, here it is, for, to my surprise, the

Editor, pointed out to us that disfigurement of staff employees, something, also evident, even sometimes, in the polity, was the heartfelt problem, something it need not be.

Now that is a surprise, if any, but what might sound strange, is that Buddha, if not Plato, thought of it first, and was presumably long heralded a lunatic for the insight, but was he wrong? Of course not.

Some say, Plato had said that poor looks or ugliness was the personification of evil, whereas some Buddhist literatures says, more kindly, that it comes from anger in a previous life. But the crucial point is this: Disfigurement can be overcome if future lives is true, something, Rebirth, that is, western science is beginning to accept.

Nevertheless, Buddhists say good looks, the opposite, comes from kindness, again, from a previous life. Which means, all of us can be good looking in future lives if we are kind now – and what if we could live one day on – forever – like this without recourse to plastic surgery for an improved look?

Either way, let us help, rather than harm people suffering from poor looks!

To do this, the following model might help.

If both material reality and mind are moving to the end of suffering, Buddha's purpose for mind, then that would equal Heaven- where good looks would be at the pinnacle. But, achieved, if we want, though not necessarily, to include Buddhism and Hinduism, achieved, that is, over life episodes!

The thing to do, for those suffering from poor looks, if this model is suitable, is to say, without fear, that however much I suffer, I will continue to act in a way that is generous, kind, compassionate etc, and then do it, like Gandhi did in the Indian independence movement.

Now Changing Faces, the charity that deals with disfigurement in the UK, said they understood where I was coming from, but couldn't comment on philosophy. Thankfully, their task, they said, is to help people who suffer from it, either at birth or after a fatal accident or through cancer, and help them get on with their lives and cope with their feelings, a much needed service.

But this long-term perspective, offered by Buddhism, is also useful.

For it shows that the moral factor in the philosophy of beautiful looks is not fatalistic, but that there is hope for those suffering from disfigurement or poor looks, to overcome their agony, and to do so over the life episode process particularly – unless we can live on, eventually, with scientific advancement, and eastern philosophy, then another method is warranted.

Is it time for 'The Psychological Revolution'?

To get to You-Valuism requires psychological advancement. The end of war warrants a psychological shift, globally, too, but how? Gandhi was selfless true, but many other countries and civilisations lag behind. Even socialism isn't about selflessness, only cooperation and love, but we need more, to make it a selfless world and kindlier.

We've had the hazardous industrial revolution, the technological revolution, the cultural revolution in China, and, in some places, to some extent, not fully, the socialist revolutions. But is it time now for - The Psychological Revolution - both in the east and other potentially you-value developing regions, and beyond?

An array of awards splashed out incessantly to the elite of diverse professions is rarely treasured for those in the psychological field. However, does the discipline deserve better, and is innovation by psychologists essential, now, more than ever?

Even the binary to unitary to Zero rook of the Buddhists needs expansion so that the twice, good/bad mind frame can develop, in actioning, to a one, just good, virtuous climate before spiralling to a Zero space of peace and emptiness – ongoing!, without losing vigour and zeal for a knowing capacity beyond this atrue.

Paul Farmer, Chief Executive of Mind, Britain's top mental health charity, says, the lack of parity between mental health and physical health has long been a key issue, though there is a sense that this is beginning to change.

Britain's Health and Social Care Act 2012, he says, enshrines in law the principle that mental health should be given equal importance to physical health, and the NHS Mandate launched recently means the NHS Commissioning Board is held accountable for ensuring these words are turned into actions.

But mental health services have always been underfunded and overlooked, he adds, saying that, the people using those services have therefore lost out as a result.

Some say that we are all mentally ill until we overcome delusion, greed and hatred. In one religion, that is – Buddhism - where health of mind is seen as the root cause of many ills, not money or ideology.

As such, does conflict begin in the mind? And so do theories like the Clash of Civilisations which deem that people's cultural and religious identities will be the primary source of conflict in the post-Cold War world only resemble this?

One in four people in the UK alone are mentally ill, annually, with one in hundred thought to be hearing voices, a symptom of schizophrenia, according to official figures. Sometimes treated as criminals, mental health bodies there are calling for greater care for patients in police custody, but does this book show there is more to it?

In the "developing world," standards are even poorer, some say, but not top Buddhists, who have a cure even for schizophrenia, they say.

But what scope is there for breath-taking innovation in psychology (and psychiatry) to bring an end to the epidemic of mental imbalance, nationally and internationally, and can governments play a role in this by administering – A Psychological Revolution!?

Quite recently, we heard from the British prime minister about the launch of a new "Longitude Prize". The £1m top prize is, he said, intended to help the search "for the next penicillin, aeroplane or world wide web", according to a BBC report. Lord Rees, the Astronomer Royal, then, the report said, will head a "Longitude Committee" to judge ideas.

But should innovations in psychology, be a, if not the, governmental high-priority, at present, world-wide, and would this lead, ingenuously, to new discoveries, or indeed methods, in the field?

Professor Pam Maras, Professor of Social and Educational Psychology, University of Greenwich, London, thinks this is possible.

She says that most social and behavioural issues can be understood by drawing on evidence from research in psychology and examples can be found across a spectrum from environmental behaviour to youth and adult aggression and anti-social behaviour.

She believes that governments are now starting to recognise the role psychology can play in contributing to innovative solutions to social problems but says whether this will lead to new discoveries is a broader question.

Though it is fair to speculate on the basis of proof so far this could well be the case, she says optimistically.

The United Nations Of South Asia

The difference between The United States model for South Asia vis-à-vis The United States of America is this: The USA speaks one language and has a common history, but South Asia is disparate, containing many different languages and ethno-national units, which means thinking outside the box is both necessary and desirable.

It is for this reason that I speak of a United Nations Of South Asia and not a United States, but the message is the same. If the United States can have fifty one - states - as part of its Union, then why can't South Asia have just as many, if not more – nations - within its geographical arena?

But is this feasible?

The well-respected Australian journalist, John Pilger, says, in one article, that the US, in particular, but, I add, the state system generally, wants, he says, to see a state of "permanent conflict" in collusion with media outlets, to fend of what Pilger describes as the real enemy – the Public!

For this, reason, wars are repeated, almost in designer fashion.

If true, this is why, for South Asia, a model of unification, not just independence and separation, is required. And this does seem to tally with, in Sri Lanka, on the surface, the sudden emergence of Muslim-Sinhala tension, almost immediately after the Tamil conflict ended.

But is it necessary, truly?

I think not.

The problem with public agitation towards state authorities, is that state actors may fear opening up more honestly, and instead rely on more historic divide and rule, and Machiavellian tactics, to keep the public at bay, and buttress up the political establishment. Which is why this article aims to help, rather than harm those with state power, without renegading on what is good for ordinary citizens – worldwide!

So far, the debate has been on "A United States Of South Asia," not "The United Nations Of South Asia", a key difference in how the conflicts there can be settled within a unified framework.

So is this possible, and would it lead to new directions in thinking on South Asia's future?

In one article, even as far back as October 2011, it was reported that Afghan President Hamid Karzai envisioned a borderless South Asia based on the European Union, which was free from violence and turmoil, saying if Europe could do it, South Asia could too. But, the paradigm stays within the United States of South Asia model, something I'm challenging here.

In that article, the reporter says the prospect, is, in any case, far off, largely because of the animosity between states like India and Pakistan. But this is capable, perhaps, of being transcended, if the political will exists and the people remain generous to the cause, however transitory it may be.

Yes, many people recognise that withdrawing colonialists left inappropriate state structures to the social realities when departing and that has fuelled nationalist uprisings in South Asia and beyond. But this can be overcome. The simple shift from "states" to "nations" can make for a United "Nations" Of South Asia that is innovative, fresh and new to the kind of polities we see operating in the world system today – even within a you-value world and region where it lead, presently, but not everlasting, because other can follow, and have, in respects, most notably Britain where welfare is second to none, despite some hiccups and problems persisting, where we should not renegade from!

Of course, ultimately all individual are intrinsically beyond national identities. The purity of mind, at its core, is something all beings possess, and so is beyond egotistical conventions like gender, nation or race. But, for the time being, can the unity between the nations of South Asia, as it exists as a social phenomena, be accomplished, by changing the focus to national unity in the region, rather than state unity?, without losing you-value in society and politics.

STRATEGY, LEADERSHIP AND YOU-VALUISM!

After all this talk on You-Valuism, let's say a bit about strategy. "Leadership is knowing where you are, knowing where you want to be, and deciphering the path of how to get there, if you want to follow a path" – Benjamin De Silva.

This is what the Lord Buddha did. He knew there was suffering. He wanted to discover the end of suffering. And he worked out the path, as he saw it, to get to it – peace. In a passage from one book on Buddhism, The Buddha's Ancient Path, the Buddha himself is portrayed as having recognised this.

It says the Buddha made clear the difference between a fully enlightened one (himself) and the Arahant, the accomplished saints who successfully take Buddhism to its end. It quotes him as saying: "The Tathagata (him), O' disciples while being an Arahant, is fully enlightened. It is he who proclaims a path not known before, he is the knower of a path, who understands a path, who is skilled in a path. And now his disciples are way-farers who follow in his footsteps. That, disciples, is the distinction, the specific feature which distinguishes the Tathagata, who being an Arahant is fully enlightened, from the disciples who are freed by insight."

A similar perspective is expressed in the book Maximum Leadership, in which the world's leading CEO's share their strategies for success. In it, it reveals five broad approaches to leadership after interviewing these CEOs.

1. The Strategic Approach
2. The Human Assets Approach
3. The Expertise Approach
4. The Box Approach
5. The Change-Agent Approach

The first of these, The Strategic Approach, it describes as the approach in which "the chief executive says he manages for success by acting as the company's top strategist, systematically envisioning the future and specifically mapping out how to get there," the same as we've outlined, more or less, above.

In business, of course, the motivation is different, often: focussing the bulk of energy on becoming the market leaders of tomorrow, it says. Unlike Buddhism, too, strategic CEOs, Maximum Leadership explains, believe they add most value by using - long-term - strategy formulation to inform every aspect of the company's business system – not being fully with the present necessarily. However, notable brands such as Dell, Coca-Cola and Deutsche Bank are categorised as among those using "the strategic approach".

The strategic approach, these executives assert is not management by gut, or intuition, or the kind of imaginative thinking associated with business visionaries such as Henry Ford or Walt Disney. It is, instead, systematic, dispassionate and structured analysis of what is called in business jargon a company's point of departure and its point of arrival, and carefully forging the path between them, it continues.

"It is the rigorous and continuous examination of an organisation's capabilities and its market context. It is, ultimately, a determination where and what a company must be to compete in the future, and how to get there faster and better than anyone else." Now this is a far cry from Buddhism, where intuition is key, or the kind of you-value politics that we've been concerned with in previous articles, a spiritual politics that goes beyond both capitalism and communism. But the leadership point is the same: knowing where we are, knowing where we want to be, and knowing the path of how to get there is an essential part of the leadership qualities required to make You-Valuism a reality if we want it peacefully without a spark trouble because it is selfless, the path to no no value left because of unlimited selfless acts practised by everybody.

The Economics of Selflessness

The BBC reported long ago that the UK jobs market continued to improve in the then three months to April, although the rate of wage increases slowed sharply, according to official figures. But, that the quarterly rate of earnings growth, including bonuses, slowed to 0.7% from 1.9% the previous month. Unemployment and earnings, as a factor of economic worth, is well established, but how would it fare in an economy that was not capitalist but selfless in tone?

Looking ahead, I have heard of the economics of limitless but not the economics of selflessness. In the former, it is said that generosity is the cause of wealth and because everyone has unlimited potential to be generous, then the amount of wealth that can be generated is also limitless.

So what is the economics of selflessness?

In an article in The Economist, entitled 'The origins of selflessness', an interesting point is made regarding economics and religion.

It states: ...."Dr Henrich also, however, found that the sense of fairness in a society was linked to the degree of its participation in a world religion. Participation in such religion led to offers in the dictator game that were up to 10 percentage points higher than those of non-participants."

It goes on: "World religions such as Christianity, with their moral codes, their omniscient, judgmental gods and their beliefs in heaven and hell, might indeed be expected to enforce notions of fairness on their participants, so this observation makes sense."

"From an economic point of view," and this is crucial, "therefore, such judgmental religions are actually a progressive force. That might explain why many societies that have embraced them have been so successful, and thus why such beliefs become world religions in the first place."

In another academic abstract, online, a health-related website, headed: 'Selfish or selfless? The role of empathy in economics', it says: "Empathy is a longstanding issue in economics, especially for welfare economics, but one which has faded from the scene in recent years. However, with the rise of neuroeconomics, there is now a renewed interest in this subject. Some economists have even gone so far as to suggest that neuroscientific experiments reveal heterogeneous empathy levels across individuals."

But it adds: "If this were the case, this would be in line with economists' usual assumption of stable and given preferences and would greatly facilitate the study of prosocial behaviour with which empathy is often associated. After reviewing some neuroscientific psychological and neuroeconomic evidence on empathy, we will, however, criticize the notion of a given empathy distribution in the population by referring to recent experiments on a public goods game that suggest that, on the contrary, the degree of empathy that individuals exhibit is very much dependent on context and social interaction."

Both fairness and empathy are useful in assessing how an economy should be selfless. However, selflessness means in essence, here, giving to others without anticipation of a return, a well-known concept in Buddhism and other religions.

Still, it is possible for one to get something back from a selfless economy since if everyone is giving freely without expectation, then a happier will by nature rebound to you, no matter what your predicament. It must do.

So, whilst the economics of selflessness is without individual ego of expectant return, the condition of *all giving to all*, would produce a production system where everyone gains from everyone else, in a way that employment and earnings become a non-issue.

So, if the profit motive remains intact, no such selflessness of the economy can really operate within those structures, even if aspects work alongside it. But the moment it is transcended, a new array forces will come into play, which opens up all levels of production to everyone, making the march towards a heavenly systemic production base, globally, and in the long term, reachable by all.

Will the time ever arrive when economists have to really look at this selfless economic option and make it tally with a change of nature in politics, also, a shift which moves it to a selfless polity, too, which is distinguished from the current capitalist-motivated polities across the globe at present, whether or not it should come after a socialist, co-operative-based economy, or not?

Yes, a selfless polity might have to come first, maybe not, but voices, schizophrenic, say, no estimate, that You-Valuism in the polity, if heralded, would take about 7000 years to come in and establish. So that makes it prepared for roughly an entrance in year 2024. If true, that is when a You-Valuist economy of selflessness should follow!

The You-media of the future

Please believe. I want it in. There's no other way, to take it on, the suffering that delivers us each time we weep. Don't worry, we'll win. With a world media news platform that heralds the end of suffering, in every way, which it fails to do, now, not just in conflict resolution, but in every way.

Is suggest an _Earth-Line-News_ title, that spans You-Valuism, but for the whole of the Earth, if it is alive, and sure, where even wind breathes and everyone wins if it is on a 'You' – true!

This is a You-Valuist media, selfless at heart, envisioning a way to stop the helter skelter and end it all, calmly and nicely. Let's not scorn it. There's time to develop, but it must try hard to end war and misery, without emotional or friendly return, and win it for us, 'a disappearance into happiness and peace of mind' – The Ultimate Truth.

The profit-driven media needs to recapitalise, this time morally, and we need advertising to match – moral marketing, again, so all is kept a win for everyone, which means politically it is not half-baked, nor just cooperative, but editorially selfless all the way through, for no false return of Nirvana for everyone.

Let's listen to everyone, even religious combatants, because they too have their story. But we mustn't compromise on selflessness, because that is where it's at, happily and constructively. You-Valuism, the path to the politics of selflessness has, with it, a religious edge, which even all Muslims can relate to, a religiosity which matches a deliverance of non-evil, because it's the highest stage of the political process, as a You-value symbol of hope and non-despair.

Let's not care if it all slumps too soon, there is time, and we will win. We need hope and forgiveness so everyone can be at peace. Let's not loose. All is up for this development to You-Valuism, and the media must follow, unscared and unbiased, because that is the path for political development laid out here, and it fits every religious and morally-leaning interest group in society, without bother.

Let's win. A resurgence of the media to a selfless abode, not unwilling to win it for us, the move to a selfless society, a shift that can win, and grace the earth, if all is just trying its path without the macro picture borne in mind. Let's really win the media non-frenzy but clam for a brighter world, with no more lost hope and reduce the tension because we'll all gain if there is a You-Valuist media globally.

This is path's end, and it tallies with a religious fervour, so we can acclaim the Muslims, if we try, for their part in a lower evil world in scriptures and sermons, and the west also has a strong history of service and compassion to others in certain segments, including with Christianity. So, let's be, and make the effort to transcend capitalism and socialism and derive a truly selfless world through the world media, even partially, for now, while capitalism is in place.

Let's look up, and keep pride, so we can win the furthest elimination of dire poverty and greed until all is soothed and free from torture and mockery. There will be a time when a You-Valuist media dominates the Earth, and we should begin by introducing media of this kind to the world gradually but without hesitation or doubt.

South Asian immigrants could import You-Value society to Britain!

The Telegraph's Bruno Waterfield's revelation that EU migrants may need a lower wage monthly to apply for asylum, is stacked to the brim. But, the contrary argument goes towards Indian influx of workers or students, say the government. Why? They say it's due to the high economic performance. But, there is another reason, underlying if not apparent.

But Bruno Waterfield's climax is not grim. How can we prosper, if our value-system is not smart? And hover on without fear of arrest? We can't! But there's more to it. No one expects South Asia to be loyal to Britain at first. But can it be? Perhaps so! But first we have to work the South Asian persona.

Of late, we expected Ed Miliband to top the cards by appearing on our You-Value interview slot. But this climax didn't come, albeit without worry, unlike the wars of past, where You-Value ethics are a miss and don't run wildly and certain. Dragging on in the abyss, where refugees often come from. So, who are they? Those lost children, of war ravaged Sri Lanka and Kashmir, or anyone else who tops the table for an asylum card to the UK from South Asia – truly, in essence, even ideally so?

I say YOU! Meaning? Why not see, if compassion is in, in them all the way through, even if their politics hasn't topped the mark yet, but could do. Can you be sure, that they will win, for Britain? I think so, but how? if they are not conscious of their own colour or political potential. Ed may be wrong to burst the bubble, but let's keep it slim. Is South Asia, of brown colour origin, especially, though not only, You-Value in persona, not selfishly aligned to their own country or abode, and how can we tell?

The idea that political society is moving to a You-Value framework, globally, is new, but not for Labour, vis-à-vis Conservative. Mainly because there are two steps up for the latter, but only one for the Labour party. Ditching 'me' in plural on capitalism, the selfish gene, may not whither away kindly or afast.

But the 'us' of New Labour cooperation, is finer still. Me, Us, You is the evolving game in politics, and Labour is closer still. Be it, unhappily, so far, though not without seeming true, let' say.

For some, the third world is lagging behind "superior" western philosophy. But is it? The You-Value ethics of South Asia is prime, and not only. All their philosophies speak of a wiser trump. Selfless is key, which is 'You' in persona, not 'Me', or a lesser, 'I'.

So this is it. Leave it in, the selflessness of You-Valuism in the political genre, unheard of in the British polity which cherishes socialism, a copy of the China syndrome? Well, not quite. But could be. But rare is it, to view South Asia as a key ally, where colonialism once triumphed!

Could South Asia be the lead political player, one day, where a you-value service economy could reign higher, if it chose to, rather than profit, or the love-cooperation syndrome of socialism? Yes, we can see it. The political system reflects the value one, and You-Valuism is the highest. Where all will lead, one day, if not now. And South Asia brown tops it, in potency not achievement yet. And so, can Britain align, in one way or another, if more refugees have to seep through on a run. So, let's not ditch South Asians as migrants first off, or willow in their pity, if they are strong. If they come, Britain could merit. And be the first You-Value society in Europe, or further afield, to benefit. Let's keep the cards open and see if they will make Britain better.

Let's dim 'You' in You-Valuism

Publicity dares, but persona wares. Let's not worry about You-Valuism. Let's be grateful, without worry or fear. That's the message of You-Valuism, the persona is not it, who claimed it, who thought of it. It's just that simple. Act and it will come true. Not worry about who did it!!

Let's talk about it somewhere not everywhere. Ed Miliband did when he said "Your Britain" to audiences up and down the country. Let's not worry about it. Let's let the publicity dim. Ed Miliband isn't. He wants to allow people a true voice in deciding the leadership contest without being full leaders. Now that's not an aspect of "You" in You-Valuism. Right that does it. He has to start stealing all my policies. Well Margaret Thatcher thought of it first – self-leaders, without grumble.

So, let's dim, not Ed, but the author of You Valuism, whoever did it, as a step closer to 'Us', the category of the socialists, a step up from 'me' in das capital and 'I'. So let's dim properly. It's not who did, but what's it about. So, let's dim all the way, get AIDA: Action, Interest, Desire, Action, a well-known marketing slogan. It happens to everyone. They keep it thin. You bring it out. Action, Karma. The world works that way, but not ought to. Then don't make it a slavery token. Make it slim. Because selflessness, or the politics of it, isn't about slavery, but a compassionate snog. So, don't take others' toll. Let's steal it, to victory, and keep it snug up, to retake it slim, again, until we win over a no murderous toll. The end of killing is the game we play, and so should you. Buddha did. He made it an eightfold way, all the way through to no death of you. So, let's follow, even with all this gripe in. No let's not whiter, but go with lifelness. The desire to live, if all else follows. Which it would, if you focus on the You-Valuist message, not the persona. Not who's behind it, but activate it, in practise. Forget all the marketing, it all stinks, even Buddha did, as persona. No flowery words he thought. We don't need it. And nor should you. Be humble. Be kind, be true, and realise your own thoughts, without worry, or at all, so we can all live on happily, forever, sometime, true. Not unkind and stigmatised. Be brave. And we shall see. All is not lost. But don't rely on me. Be aware. Don't take it wrong. Be wise.

It's not who created You-value that is it, it's why. So forget who ever authored it, and it will work, even without the long over-work, which is required to make it tick. Be a nice guy. Cover ill intent. It stinks. Have less coverage of it, and just make it stick. Has Ed? So be a nice guy to him, as well as Cameron, and the other present and past party leaders. They all make U-turns, as Buddhism in Western Australia outlines.

Why Marxism failed in South Asia - So far!

Now start a no-war! Jurisprudence doesn't work if all is on a You. Now let's talk. Maybe, if all is said undone, there is scope for Marxism in a you-value framework, which South Asia is - near. But not fully. Marxism is a step higher than capitalism, but you-value ethics is more grateful. Don't succumb to the kingly dare, but Marxism is not higher still than You-Valuism.

Now take care. Cooperation lasts, but selflessness sparks. Don't dwell. Just see, not only be, for a higher value framework, with nothing especially in, which is empty. No need to rush. Just act slim. Don't hum You-Valuism, only spark it. Ignite selflessness. Don't over wane, only not complain. Just keep it near, so all can comprehend, where it all leads. To a selfless you-value unterribly unscorned reality of all for all.

Let's leave it there. Some don't care. Except for those, those who see Marxism as happier all over than capitalism, an 'us'-based production system, competitive and neat, before the 'you'-type, which South Asia didn't see. Until now. Yes, we'll see, if it conquers all round. That's true. Keep neat. That's our sight. That Marxism didn't work because the You-value ethics of selflessness, intrinsic to the region, took precedence of 'us' and revolution, unless it warrants, with not dictatorship and over authoritarian – but strikes and riots.

So, that explains, how all the religions, South Asia bound, took a start-lead off bounds for Marxism with Naxalites and the JVP in Sri Lanka, which still cherishes our way, but not fully. Yet. Which it can be, no do. So let's let them in, the selfless way. Let's not worry if all doesn't work through, and South Asia remains less selfish, instead of selfless. But it ought to, the next stage in political development, which even the Orientals have clung to, religiously – not yet fully mature, is, still – Marxism.

But the West and Africa need to follow, not unwarrant it, but decipher through, until all is not meaningless, but through. So let rebirth and Karma spread, to the West, and Africa until all can see the Deathless or Lifefull way/s. Which earnest in proper

perspective as to our plight on earth, making it bigger, not in heart, but persona, non-marketive but transparent, until all is clear.
That's when no bicker between Capitalism and Marxism need apply, because there is something bigger here, not at stake, but to carry on – unmurderously. Because we need not war, only a heart. So let's let it stick, not improper but only sound, in tune and fine. This is the way of Marxism true. But You-Valuism is even higher, not better, until it sticks.
This is our heap, the heap of added value, not in business, but in society, where politics can follow, not implement until it's right - necessarily. So take care, and be merry. Give to others and see. Buddha made his rook stick. But is it a Deathless to no life, or life in – which warrants lifefulness. Let's see, without abode, only wiser. Let's be. And sing. Sing the Deathless or Lifefull view which is a You-Valuist tune in politics.
So let's unharrow, and be freer!

Defeating Fascism with a World Military

((This article was written using visual data meditation (Divine Eye maybe) and the voices of schizophrenia and was published in Ceylon Today publication receiving over 600 views.))

The rise of Fascism in Europe, right now, is a warning. Fascist regimes have won power democratically in the past. The threat remains, as economies struggle, and command over national militaries, in just one country, is all they need, to resurface.

Could a world military body, instead of NATO, help us go beyond national interest politics, of this kind, where states are prone to Fascism, compete for power and economic gain, and, on the contrary, help establish a more human, co-operative and service/knowledge-driven global world order?

The idea is intrinsically already of interest to individual, country-based militaries, who die needlessly in endless conflict, with national-government-based decisions, fuelled on sometimes shared, intelligence information.

One option is to make the national militaries, as one, the military arm of the United Nations. However, it should be independently investigated to prevent human right abuses, both individual and, crucially, social.

The national militaries, for now, until merged, can be a subsidiary of a world military body, in this way. It should have all colours and races belonging to it. NATO can be replaced. A world military should take precedence over national interests.

With a rotational leadership, not just one, it should be a subsidiary of civilian leadership. It won't come together, however, unless everyone joins. It could also be a joint complimentary reserve to Interpol, the international police. Its primary role: To protect the Earth.

Still, it's not on the agenda at all, however, it's more tangible, in the short term, from the thinking of the far left, where changing the whole economic system is the pre-requisite for change.

The first thing is that this is easy, and would help transform militaries into a civilian role, rather than combat, as it is world-wide. It would also avert rogue or dissident states unilaterally using national militaries against its own population, if led by an individual authority, rather than a country.

The shift: the military is no longer an instrument of politics, but of service. Eventually, it could lead to no military on the planet, if countries and people follow suit. Its feasibility, at present, not far, if people and politicians follow through.

A world military is already near with NATO, the UN and our very own One World concept. Yes, and it will also help defeat Fascism for good. National governments can monitor it, until world government presides. One World, or, in the end, just One Love? No longer the desire of states, as its call, but the service of personnel.

Yes, a world military may have to continue a combat role in some areas, until civilian rule dominates the whole world, beyond national borders, but the strength of a world military command would make it less appealing for sub-state actors to rebel, unless existential conditions force their hand. Which is why human rights have to go alongside one military, to prevent this from occurring.

Not only would a world military stop us sparring, intermittently, but would also help us to overcome national and cultural identities. It would help us conquer other planetary zones, if life on Earth perishes, and would help us counter outer-terrestrial invasions, should they occur in future.

Yes, Africa can be in, with its own world military wing. It will help naught poverty, as no one would want to mess with it. That would reduce economic insecurity. It will increase the confidence that we can win, as a species.

In the current climate, sub-state nationalities could also have access to the protection of a global military, which would improve cultural relations, like with the Tamils and Palestinians. And, the imperial to and fro would no longer be required, because we'll all win in one way or another.

Ultimately, it's just people that count, not nations, civilisations or political loyalties - and the police can help.

YOU-VALUE COPS!

Don't run. The police are, in Britain, a tiger lineage origination, over Rebirth, our meditations reveal, true or false, if they use camouflage, the greatest defenders of the Earth, who sit and stalk and follow through to their dare without wishing through like the rest of us do?

Marx said the police were an "instrument of the state" but we say not. Their moral prestige is higher than the rest of man, we indulge, cos it's easy to attack others when we're safe. But, not so easy when in trouble, like we all are from time to time.

Being morally superior is not an easy task, in the rough and tumble of the job, but it shook us to see how far the police can go to save a guy, and it's untrembling me. So be neat like Tiger dare are, but not all police forces are this way as Tiger, we see.

In Sri Lanka, we say that python line up is the attack, with tiger and chimp lineage in the polity, but that's not to say it's for worse, only a different way, if right. The police, whatever animal spring they arise from, are in a difficult job, but we prey when they fail to turn up, but we can't let them loose the way, in an Earth pit, where all the climate could change if we're better on it – that's a choice. Yes, it could be, that the Earth's gravitational weather and trauma field with earthquakes and volcanoes dries up when we act less selfishly as a whole, unsure, but the Tsunamis of late only hit murderous regions in guerrilla warfare. A coincidence or not?

And the police are also affected, if true, so we expect the best service from them, whether we like them or not, which we do, because they help us daily and always have done. Yes, the police may be superior morally than the rest of the crowd, and we can win with them, if we agree to surrender our arms, and knives, and live happily without any divide tactics even or as well here on Earth, which come from self-division historically and buttressed by my own conversations with monks over the years.

Not a surprise that the police are investigators through and through, so we expect a past life connection to the Buddhist monks region, or aka The Sangha, or a link to outer terrestrial realms in Rebirth which practise, meditations, say, again, military warfare. We are on an up. The police are neatly lit, again, and highly specialised and should be forgiven for mistakes so they can delve into higher morality like the rest of us, if they were near past life monks or nuns before.

A You-Value world needs them, and we shall win. Yes, we need the police and like them and want them neater than the rest, but they require their reputation in tact. A You-Value polity should make the police a top priority, and we shall see the test if South Asia follows through one day. The You-Valuist ideal is the front political runner, we say, the top ladder of spirituality and selflessness and the police should lead the way.

Seeing the last of No-Self!

The western tradition in philosophy has left an indelible scar on the notion of what it is to be an individual in this world. But what has been left out is that the individual, due to danger and the lost soul, has re-lost what it means to be an alone in a decrepit society. On one rook, the Buddhist concept of No-Self means to have "no individual essence" and this is what is left when people get trapped in power games without a selfless abode, where people can't live freely and in one with nature, and in understanding with what nature is all about.

Locke was who transformed the individual from society and saw that it worked in business with a love of money, but it had little idea, his philosophy, what the implications would be of individuals in terms of their natural essence and how it worked in the business of life.

Opposing No-Self, if you have to, not always, in other understandings of the concept, is to return to a natural state of being, a oneness, no wholeness of self with nothing missing so our personality is left in tact, without worry of outside interference or distaste of life.

[The voices say] The Earth was delivered to allow people of evil origin, now not that we all are, only started off like this, to live in a world where our actions returned the repercussions from the natural world and social and individual world, until we can learn to live as one with harmony and not non-grace, and Karma and Rebirth fit in to this picture gracefully, not without true!

[They continue]…this is why this universe was formed as black for evil (black energy) until light, which is now day, and karma, later added, was the vehicle with which we learned to do no wrong because of the hit from the social world. Rebirth adds on, further, saying you have another chance.

The funny things is, inflation in science, where the universe expands rapidly since its origin may be an internal Karmic turn in the universe which the scientists left out, which allow new planets to form if a social grouping develops sufficient life mass energy to be plumped on its own therein over Rebirth or before.

But the positive side is: If actions are good, and people given choice so not compelled - the reason for the evil start - then new

planetary horizons or stars could emerge that take on new, "good"
life forms, where all is right, more peaceful and nice.

Just a hypothesis for the scientists to discover, if they will take on
this new formulation for the reason for our existence and the
accelerated pace of the universe and the formation of new stars
peacefully.

But it was Buddhism, on Earth, for now, which provided a strategy
to evolve the mind to the point of "no turmoil", so empty, you just
live on, peacefully, with no death of you (The Deathless) so
Rebirth can end once your reach eternal life over to Heaven,

So, this was the start of life, said earlier, in this universe, the big
bang as they say in science, we see, so that it makes it abundantly
clear that selflessness is the way to end suffering and put an end to
No-Self, so all can live freely, with strong individual personality
brought with no terror all-round so abundantly so.

South Asians have made their way, more abundant, not perfectly
so, to this position over life episodes, we encourage, and so can
we, all of us, until all is selflessly bound not in a two-way, but
multitudinal, stream, cross-matching, by everyone, to everyone.
And this is where we should be, at end, day in day out, without
mentors, as self-explained in all the major religions.

This is what the Buddha meant by No-Self, no selflessness, in one
interpretation not unwise, thus warranting it as, perhaps, a kind of
illness that caused suffering. No one is blaming anyone for
protecting themselves by transforming in with it, with added
power not grace, if people want to know who you are, thus you
present yourself hidden as No-Self so can change. But the day
must come when it will end. When everyone is selfless, there will
be no need to hide in a No-Self show or, more likely, compulsion.
And only then, and therefore, will God's will persist! – to produce
truth-perfected being, we see!

The Non-Political!

Let's be brief. The Non-Political is just another way of saying when politics ends, and the You-Value sprit is where it should lead when it happens, a way of finalising all conflict, so not the end of communism/capitalism relations like some authors suggest, but when the whole world is selfless like the Buddha warrants, a 'You' of a final briefing, when everything ends, politically, because no one needs politics anymore.

Yeah, let's leave it there. So why worry? Well the problem is this. With so much game theory buzzing around and real politicking, even in our hospitals and mental health services, there isn't much rest for the wicked, or for those of us, who try to stimulate real discussion going, less. The West has its gambit, and some there have said they want You-Value on a spirit, not on a buzz or evangelical, like Communism, so lest keep it gradual.

A dare for a dare is its game, we see, so be brief, or you'll get caught up in a not so nice worrier not free of life, but don't complain because there are good aspects to You-Valuism, like the dole and council housing but much wider, but we've got to be fair. Earth terrestrial life, where man eats man, even in dare, is a no go in a You-value abode, which is where all life heads, if we are to create the heaven that we all want one day, without worry or torture.

It's a deathless game, or everlasting life, as the Christians want it, but with all this politicking going down, how are we to win, any of us, nicely, plainly, triumphantly. We can't. So let's not wrangle in the closet and make things open, so we can get better and overcome mental illness, the Zero way – Buddhistic, to emptiness, where everything fits, not untriumphantly, but pleasantly.

This is where it's at. Let's double politick to get it in, sooner rather than later so we can less attack, not massive, and keep things clean the godly way, until all is ream, shiny and free. This is all we have to look at as the full cycle of the politics game here on Earth, because no one wants it in explicitly, but in persona we're already there, for some.

This is game over of the selfless match, when everything is caput, not unnicely, but with a no need to go to other planetary destinations, because life here on Earth is a must, and not unfriendly, because we win in a selfless world, and it doesn't take much to get there, only sacrifice and learn, so don't get angry and make that your dare. Just wise on, and keep neatly so that we can win as a species.

That's the end of politics, and we'll know when everyone can live by their good thoughts and persona, so we don't have to go into the abyss like some envisaged was the only escape because selflessness doesn't materialise if you're wavery, and it is, if you don't' give away our negative half for the better and act up so we can all win. So, let's see the way in to a higher politics rather than just fend off the way out of life's miseries of suicide and war. Then we'll all be winners!!!

You-Valuism in a global context!

Can people like Rajapaksa, then President of Sri Lanka, now, when this was written, be a saviour to mankind and lead the way, and as his successors, without creating a race war, by making You-Valuism the sole, lead, not ideology, but agenda, in the polities of mankind, by going higher than Communism, as in Marx, as the pinnacle, or not, in theory?

Critics say, successive governments in Sri Lanka of past have used Buddhism as a guise, only superficially, as a non-attachment and inclusion of reality, as much of the way, but I say they have failed to see that selflessness is the key, the main non-culprit to a higher reality on the ground, and politically, which takes us further to a more nicer world, where all can live earnestly and as one.

It does not matter that other social realities and polities lag behind, at present, for the moment, but it can alter when conditions arise, dependent origination, as they say, often, in Buddhism, because it is the value structure of 'no' to 'us' that we must decipher and get beyond.

To repeat, the existential philosophy of life as meaningless is a 'no' meaning to life remit and the next step up, capitalism, is a 'me' value culprit or reward, depending on where we are in the ladder, social. But communism, or back to socialism, for safe is an 'us' cooperative slant. So only You-Valuism, can mount the final nail in the value structure, which is a 'you' value philosophy, again, and has to be, if we are to see clearly the value progression in societies as a systematic whole, and we must.

It might sound odd to give a new name for a polity that doesn't exist, but if the oppression of Tamils was a reality in Sri Lanka one time, and even, some say, now, until we hope, it dissolves, not adds on, then we must admit that selflessness must be the key ingredient in all South Asian philosophies for polity development.

We must win. If this type of polity, selfless, doesn't exist now, then it should do, to keep away all the faults of other systems, and if we accept responsibility for a higher polity, in type, in South Asia, then that should pave the way for other polities, globally, to follow suit one day, not through revolution, or social upheaval, necessarily, or it could come the other way.

But when the social realities in those countries correspond to this type of polity, and it will, one day, then we will take a higher ground to a more compassionate world hereon in.

The day will come, we hope, when people power will meet social stability and no more need for revolution or social unrest, because You-Valuism is a higher world order which can win for all, cross-culturally, as well as globally, throughout polities of a lower order like Communism tried to arrest but was defeated in some.

However, we do not need violence or demonstrations to accomplish it because when people are selfless in themselves, then the political realities will change automatically, if that's the way it has to turn. I'll leave it there for a global audience to consider and hope they will see the merit in it for once without violent disorder. Let's keep and be slim.

Not all polities, nonetheless, need to wait for a selfless population to materialise You-Valuism because selfless encouragement along those lines, now politically, can act, in seeming cooperation, as a propeller to a brighter future, but lets keep it, again, slim to see what happens in any case thereof.

YOU-VALUISM HOUSE

Yes, we need a vision and You-Valuism does it. We need it quick, and neat. Just be cool. There is no way to win except with non-worry. Do your best to make it work – You-Valuism all the way to a persona that is justified and real.

Don't run away. All we need is a climax of non-graft when all is social, but there is a higher way of selflessness all the way in to a philosophy of *The Way In*, here, near and right. So, get there, fine and merry, if you can.

Don't worry about me, however harsh it may seem because we all need a space to work in, and so does You-Valuism, which is why we recommend a "You-Valuism House", a political philosophy office with a marketing clout, helpful and kind, not unnice.

So let's win it, happy a free. For those of you interested, who can keep the pace, with not without know, must work at it, for a freer ride, all the way to Heaven, if it is in futuristic. Now no, don't go too far, with all this worry near us, we have to work for better even if no Heaven causes trouble.

Be good to me, and help us on with a you-value house, and try it soon, like rock n roll, yes, that's there, in, neat and merry, because we're the best at it in London, new visions that keep and we need the resources to win.

So, get there, and send us your offers to ISHI at go on i_desilvauk@yahoo.co.uk and remember don't be afraid because nothing's going wrong in Karmaland which is where we're at, so we need you there too, generously and kind, if generosity brings prosperity and abundance for everyone in. In society strong.

So get in touch with your ideas, and make it work the You-Valuist way – to freedom!

Benjamin De Silva

The You-Valuist Party

Go on then. Let's have a You-Valuist party. Let's not look far,
even Britain and Europe need one. Let's delve into a You-Valuist
party, without triumphant or side track into Lenin and the
proletariat without leap forward on up. Let's get it strong. A You-
Valuist party is smart and non-wrong. Let's not whither, because
selflessness is not clumsy but upright.

With no hidden camera to the future, it wicks afar, not just to
Nirvana but for all religions and temperaments. Let's not run. Just
be free. Just home in, near, and you'll see, a party of this kind
ought not be far off, once the big picture surmounts in not weak
but heralds in.

No need to be far from the masses, yes all we need for starters is
the service sector, as primary, not old, but efficient and nicer
though, if it is or can be. Service is what Gandhi advocated and
Buddhists do too, but don't despair even the west do it correctly.
Peace of mind is the primary goal, apart from selflessness, the
development of mind, clear and awake. Be higher than the usual
stuff, of material want, even as a need for, but not certainly this
far. Be good. Let's be mindful or care free not but full. Aware.
And give, without expecting a return. This is the path, and the
You-Valuism polity of the future would represent it.

Let's not worry too far, but make it a goer. Its members are givers
in persona, the essence of Karma if you give more than you take,
then it will bring a higher plus, without all the deception in. Yes,
money can wane, but character has to hold strong. We need it.

The You-Valuist party are service-orientated, not cooperatives like
the USSR Marxists, and they can win because revolution need not
be the only way, except for system-change, but compassion, with
democracy in, oh no we got to hold, but patience is one of the
cardinal spiritual qualities. But cooperation is not ruled out, only
not the top notch, because selflessness is no-self fully, to start,
which means peace must just happen, as an experience devoid of
ego or personality. It just is, in process and reality, the ultimate
reality and truth of things.

Is this where the mind is heading, if the universe produced mind to
develop higher or did it? Absolute peace of mind, cultivated
through a gradual virtue training, in Buddhism, where it is neither

good nor bad, right nor wrong, it's the way it is without crumbling when things go wrong.

Peace of mind and awareness, coupled, because the conditions are there for it to go not slow but firm. An unshakable deliverance of mind, with equanimity and free. These are just some of the skills of a You-Valuist party where the bridge is selflessness, the next step up after Marxism in the political hierarchy.

The bottom line for any You-Valuist part is Wisdom, with a capital 'W' because the wise not only prosper but never wane. The real-time fellow can see it in their eyes, because only one who puts others before self, can really avoid the paranoia of the Cold War, and deliver on a free mind so that society itself is free and wholesome.

And tax need not be permanent or full unlimited. It can stop, with a limit. That way, when things go rough, new products can free of tax thereafter, a plus, needed and warranted. Please see, perception goes up with a higher value, and when it does the polity can give. Capitalism brings take, Socialism brings share, but You-Valuism brings give, in social as well as political relations, so do it. Be in – ream!

Most important, for politicians, is to overcome the stop gap of selfishness and corruption under capitalism, se be near and take all not, but some, until all is bright and non-weedy, oh I meant seedy, non-seedy, because with the advent of Socialism, things can become sharing, remember, sharing – in – the polity, because political philosophy, primary, is intra and inter-state relations and behaviour, so be in, near, and non-wrong, again, frank and kind, until all is surer, or is it uncertain? Not the You-Valuism way which is precise: "I live for anything" first, "I live for me" second, "I live for us" third, and, "I live for you" last, from Existentialism to You-Valuism – neat!!

Benjamin De Silva

You-Valuism & the liberation of the polity

The global polities need a revamp of ideas in a Karma world, because endless war/conflict and bickering is bad moral conduct under this law, with negative consequences far-reaching and wide. So how can we expect people to act virtuously, like some political philosophers wanted, in a capitalist world where competition is the norm? The politicians should lead by example. And they can – eventually.

The transition from capitalism to socialism is not yet complete, far from it, but cooperation isn't a liberation as such, except for workers, perhaps, from standard interpretations, unless in the polity. But, dare I say it, what about the politicians themselves? Can they expect a liberative life with all this legal authority leading to overt, often, turmoil, far less than happy?

The liberation of the polity, in any country, can come about from the evolution of governments from a profit/growth motive to a co-operative motive, to a selfless motive: Capitalism, Socialism and You-Valuism, respectively. Even the pre-Hindu Vedas said that selflessness was one of the paths to a higher spiritual realm, among others. 4 paths in total, actually.

So, this is how the politics of Sri Lanka and world can also go, in time to come, so that people at last receive a selfless hand from governments, not help with a money mind in the background, which it has been, even in the west, where welfare is still always tied to profit and the state of the national capitalist economies.

No, the truth is that economies can one day also become selfless, truly, but it will take time. We are no way near that stage now. Still, politicians and prime ministers can win at their own game, if they steer politics towards selflessness, because that is where the polities are heading, or could do, if socialism is the natural succession to capitalism. A step up from a me-value system, to an us-value system, and finally, with You-Valuism, to a you-value system of selflessness and non-greed.

The charity sector, so far, is the closest to a selfless economy and a lot can be learned from it even if financial considerations place limitations on how far they can act, presently. But it is a seed in the You-Valuist fruit because the industry works as a service to the under-privileged and can set the tone for a more selfless politics to come.

Could manufacturing and retail one day, centuries down the road, 70 in total till 2024, schizophrenic voices say, possibly, to get there, work, now, on a selfless basis, perhaps this is where we can get to once the self-interest drive has been superseded?

You-Valuism is where politics, economy and religion blend, to make for a safer world and one that hugs the ancient traditions of many spiritual roads the globe over. So let's get there, politically, also, because then our leaders will themselves be on a path to liberation whilst in power, according to the great scriptures of old, so they, too, reap the benefits of service, in a way that is kindlier and better for all than the current set up.

You-Valuism, is, the liberation of the polity – globally!!!!!!!!!!

Benjamin De Silva

YOU-VALUISM

Quotes from the Bible of Political Philosophy

Benjamin De Silva

This book is dedicated to my long-term love, as a teenager, a White-Asian relationship of true romance in Britain, who, deservedly, gave me the tip to make You-Valuism a reality in the field of theory by accessing the true, again, value of Marxism, which, for her, was love!

Benjamin De Silva

1. "Religions of the world merge on selflessness, that is the surest way to achieve religious peace. It is ok to have different goals or destinations, like Heaven, Paradise & Nirvana, but we can each achieve a common will".

2. "You-Valuism cannot be racist like the war-mongers. People are close to it everywhere. Even Christianity in the west preaches to give more than you receive, which renders all skin colours capable of achieving a selfless politics throughout the world map".

3. "In the spirit of Gandhi, no war can be fought with a You-Valuist agenda, it is a peaceful philosophy, political, which renders the division between religion and politics obsolete, the division has been overcome."

4. "Political philosophy, on the highest level, has so far progressed only up to co-operation, formally, but now, with You-Valuism, we can have a will that one day can include selflessness in politics, whether informally or not."

5. "Religions must still be, where correct, senior to the Socialist will, because all religions say we should give, not just co-operate, which means they have a higher theoretical position even within a world socialist order or remit."

6. "The Way In philosophy of You-Valuism reveals the way into a surer political order from: a "No-Value" politics and society, to "Me-Value" ones to "Us-Value" ones to "You-Value" societies, where people will be free to give and take without antagonism. Nice."

7. "When You-Valuism strikes, up to 7000 years from now, in estimation, we will or should have a civilian-led world military, which can itself one-day end, when people are peaceful, selfless and co-operative. It must win."

8. "You do not need You-Valuist political parties if world socialism triumphs, home grown in each country, one-country to many, internal, because world socialism is enough to muster world peace, if everyone helps each other instead of contends."

9. "True Marxism, ABSOLUTE, is co-operative personal relations between everyone everywhere, and if this comes, we will have the capacity, alongside Buddhism, as Einstein desired, to win true freedom from conflicts of every kind."

10.   "Buddha and Buddhism allows us to have peace in the mind, with awareness. This means that every rational thought we have within it, is untiresome and free. This is the essence of Buddhism, to allow mindfulness with rationality to blossom without suffering."

11. "You-Valuism can be nurtured by being selfless in small doses, by being generous and happy with it too. When we do this, we share happiness, not just keep it in. This is how to light many candles of happiness with one flame."

12. "Even international trade, or segments of it, can be selfless many centuries down the road. We may not need it, but why try? Namely, because we want to put a smile on everyone. Socialism deserves it."

13. "We need a spiritual politics in a capitalist world, so that one-day everyone will have the grain of spirituality within them. We must try. Sometimes it is difficult, like when people hate, or take revenge, but money transfer isn't alone with charity. Help win it."

14. "Sometimes, we demonstrate at evil, to change it. But we need more positive energy also. Like shows and art galleries. Make it triumphant for everyone, not just egotistical. Everyone has free choice, so use it wisely. Social Mass Energy (SME) has to be positive, more so, so use it."

15. "We need a psychological revolution to accompany You-Valuism, so that we are no longer the victims or perpetrators of abuse, but the givers of something more valuable. This change to morality in all parties of abuse, should take centre stage in all psychology soon."

16.   "A present moment or future strategy will suffice for You-Valuism in religious circles, and it will take time for Universal Selflessness to triumph. Business is like this, religions can follow suit with the spirit of morality."

17. "An economics of selflessness may not be needed, but if it comes, decades down the line, beyond Socialism, we should make it work - definitely. This means going beyond exchanging in Marxism, to just giving, a leap of ultimate perfection."

18. "Selfless media, with a You-Value spirit, is needed world-wide, so that offenders are equipped with the compassion to help them win. They too are victims. We have to make it there soon, as a segment, so the true Buddhist spirit regains momentum."

19. "Many people in the east, who flock to the west, are told repeatedly in literature to be Selfless. This must not change. When we are confronted with opposition, the religious texts inform us to be kind to our haters. Stick. Many people in the west follow this too, perhaps."

20.   "No one should, really, be pinned down as You-Valuist. It is in our actions that we be good to others, even if our being says otherwise. So let go of it as an identity, just be good, and help all peoples everywhere with a peaceful mind. Then it will work."

21.   "The politicians will be liberated to No-Self in Buddhism when they see the path, globally, to a selfless politics after Socialism as the pinnacle. When they reach it, they will have less regard to profit and more to welfare,   of   others, especially."

22.　"The workers are the army of Socialism. Let them ensure world socialism is never reversed when it arrives for mankind's benefit."

23. "When we feel happiness, it is within. When we give it, it is shared."

24.   "One study has found the name of our planet has been reversed. The Karma position of its true name, maybe to sing tunefully to a harmonious economic policy. This policy, therefore, can only mean Socialism on a world scale. Do it."

25.   "The reason for The Age Of Reason in academia can only mean that the enlightened thinkers were reasonable types who saw the causes for things and were sensible. It can only be an Age if we transmit this quality throughout society to everyone so we can all live peacefully and gracefully, without harming anyone."

26. "With Socialism and You-Valuism, we shouldn't have to survive for fitness, but can live with others and receive a hand from them willingly. Only bad right-wingers will justify ill-will instead of compassion, which they need too. Hypocritical."

27. "People expect things that aren't given, especially in war. This must end for the sake of good taste. Buddhism is the religion of taste, the Way It Is, if it's bad, ditch it, for better all the way on, until we are all healthy and fine."

28. "Many political philosophers, east and west alike, have preached Virtue as the means for happiness. This is sometimes misunderstood. It is not just our own happiness we should seek, but the happiness of others. Virtue helps it."

29. "We are not wrong if we are right, which is something German philosopher Kant allured. Buddhism upholds it too, with Right in the eightfold path. This is truth. If it is right, it is true, a theory of truth that is pertinent."

30.   "The Earth Liberation Business Plan, globally, must be the transcendence of Fascism, to Capitalism, to finally World Socialism, home-grown, then there is no need for You-Valuism necessarily. Even if we desire it."

31.　　"Seek not more, most, many or all, but seek better. Then we know we give health the priority for betterment is the basis of all health. When we feel better, it heals us, in whatever form. Health is a symbol of success."

32.　"Another option to the One-World concept is the One-Country one when separatism subsides. If we have one country here on Earth, everything will settle, and we can live on freely. That's a sure win."

33.   "We cannot just exist or sell, we need to live. Life in others is what brings beauty. Not just calm. We have to get the balance so we are not just couch potatoes, but vibrant members of society. That's where beauty lies."

34.　"One day it will be Normal for everyone to target co-operation and selfless behaviour. People know the plan now. I hear it in defence frequently, and people know the difference. Then all crime will be solved."

35.   "Give beyond your race, nation or business. We all deserve it. Life is a hard battle, so let's make the journey brighter. Not just when we are in need, but always. Be fair, just and kind. To all people of any skin colour".

36.　"What we need, all of us, is wisdom, wisdom to be good and just/fair, selfless. You-Valuism is wise, so is Socialism, don't be fools and let war win. When we recognise this, we will be wise, and when everyone is wise, there will be – UNIVERSAL WISDOM!"

37.	"The western Buddhist Sangha, order of monks and nuns, have offered so much gracefulness, it is a beacon of hope. The love and wisdom emanating from the western priests shines a ray of light on how Buddhism should be practised. Keep it up."

38. "Once we practice co-operation in our free time, we will then have built the Capacity to act co-operatively any time we will. That's the cure. The same applies to selflessness. It is a capacity we seek, and then it will return returns."

39.   "Politics will end when people are selfless and co-operative. This is the start of Socialism. It's end is unforeseen, a zero which could yield wonders far beyond our imagination. It will take many centuries, but don't give up. It can be happy and compassionate."

40. "Change the world by upgrading your value to selfless with You-Valuism. Even if not formally introduced, it means we have self-worth, the way to defeat chauvinism. Politics is the Deliverance of Value, and selflessness is the highest value, compassionate - on Earth".

Buddhism, Socialism & You-Valuism!

(50 self-made articles on the Buddhist Sangha & Socialism)

Benjamin De Silva

This book is a gift (dana) dedicated to the Western Buddhist Sangha (order of monks and nuns) by the community of hope from South Asia presently in countries of the west in gratitude of their "desire", service and response towards a new, more peaceful and kindlier world order which will be in line with all Buddhist traditions for a wider and more just peace held commonly between all sentient beings residing on Earth: Humans and animal life forms forever on.

Workers are the "*army*" of Socialism!!!

(ARTICLE 1)

Some misunderstand the Socialist dilemma: How can you have world socialism with each nation state competing for power within a nation-state-system, making foreign invasion easy? Easy. Make the workers its target as the sole benefactor and responsibility for the safety of a foreseeable socialist order, Marxist-led, which heralds its stake in the new era, by instilling in its pride the necessity for empowering themselves with the aim of defending Socialism itself prior to the national or later global army.

These were the words of Paula Right, author and journalist/top editor, after witnessing ample mistakes in Marx's (the workers' army) role in literature and speech where no mention was made of the workers of each nation-unit as being, manifold, the *army* of Socialism for all.

She said: "When business-minded colonialism insists hard on others by foe by attempting to overtake foreign states, it is normally the armed forces of the home state that tackle it, or its civilians combined, guerrilla. Not so with Socialism. Here the workers cripple or shake/"influence" the economy for the enemy, not the clientele who are indigenous or kind migrants – fair".

This is the difference between Socialism of the old kind known to us all, and, the new frontier of world Socialism wherein all borders can one-day end and the light of a borderless world with one international workers army capable of stopping and catastrophising any capitalist-led imperial effort of the few or the miserable can win!

After all, it is financial and monetary reasons, primarily, that instil cross-border rivalry anyway which the workers can worsen without jeopardising their own freedom because food and shelter can be shared! Civilians can help.

The Buddhists may know this, and call for it every day as, in combination, the 4 requisites the books and their talks often repeat!

Don't' balk at the foreseen in any rook by harping on at the defeat syndrome which says once known strategically it can be sidestepped because it's hard to do this strong if done fairly, until the threat has gone. The real idea is making people aware that foreign invasions, however underhand, are simply wrong, so stand by it. You must, if we are to win Socialism once and for all, Paula or Ms. Right repeated.

If national armies, instead, attack, in these contexts, there would-be bloodshed and loss of life for them also unfair, without warning, with gunfire, that is, now, but this need not happen with the workers army concept, so stand by the Socialist dream and make will, will for a new vision which stands out: frank, fair and right, Ms. Right astounded!

When Marx said "Workers of the world unite, you have nothing to lose but your chains" this is what he meant," Right said: "Take it on the chin when invaders attack, organise cleverly and co-ordinate with other workers in various countries to put an end to capitalist expansion instead of world socialist relations – co-operative".

Rare, but true unless it can be avoided – better, only, if it is not genocidal against the indigenous population, where more hardship may be unavoidable. Sad, but true.

So, this is what might happen one-day, predictive!, we can all win a workers' army to protect world Socialism when it arrives.

Making the workers the army, temporarily, in the then current climate, maybe it, but if it, Colonialism, post or neo, occurs, then yes, it must happen then until a new Socialist idea is encapsulated in life and practised, as of when adjusted so far that no one can stop its non-reversal for ever on world-wide!

Now that's the real workers unite idea in Marx or there abouts!, Paula warrants.

Benjamin De Silva

How my family helped me

(ARTICLE 2)

"My father encouraged me with one word when growing up, and that word is "Marxism"!

"He knew in his heart that he wanted my take, as a bright young lad, on Socialism and the Marxist ladder".

She added: "It took me until 45 to make my first book related to the subject. When I was young I used it defensively, to stop fights, because I knew it would bring in to the action something bigger, and more dignified, so bullies listened, for not knowing what it was. They usually stopped attacking. It kind of worked".

Paula Right was bred in London and hiked on about Marxism her whole life, virtually, until fifty at least, but there was never a pause because her father wanted Socialism and nothing else despite a brief pause to help in Sri Lanka, before returning to it on Facebook with a nice brand of Marxist titles.

Her parents were Buddhist in theoretical leaning, which encourages that service for money is ok, not bad, but they knew, well, her father did, that only Socialism could solve his money problem for good. But no one ever listened. Except Paula! And they won, with her first title on You-Valuism - The idea of a selfless politics structurally!

This authorship showed clearly two things mainly: That transient leanings towards Marxism and Socialism were right in the wider scheme of things, and, implicitly, that half of the world's population had already reached a spiritual stage that had transcended Socialism or hit the spot anyway or in some way at least.

Her mother, however, in true female spirit, knew she had to be practical and keep the finances tight and secure, for now and for future, even yelling and attacking Paula when young to comply. She knew she had no choice in a capitalist world, and things were harsh!

It was this schizophrenic dilemma that made Paula tough. She knew she had to help on both fronts. "My mother was fierce and reared me like a lion. But my father was gentle, and strong. Both leaned on me for support in different ways, and I knew I had to supply worthwhile stuff for each of them."

This made her insane. But it worked. She now studies Marxism with an eye on financial security until Socialism triumphs, a risk many people are not willing to take, yet! There are some, many, who study Marxism but are capitalists through and through, which makes them corrupt. Paula is not one of them which is why she figured out what Marxism and other ideologies were in reality, in actuality.

She defines it!

1. Marxism - The "targeting" of co-operation in personal relations everywhere
2. Socialism - The economics and now politics of cooperation in shops (business) and the polity
3. Communism – The "accomplishment" of co-operation on all levels: culture, media even sport etc

Paula, or Ms Right, when more mature, explained to her dad that the point of Marxism is to be "Co-operative Free" as the starting point, which means you practise with it so much it vanishes up so you don't have to think about it anymore, it just happens – the end of Karma in that field.

Dad was kind of right! That's how to change the world by changing the moral impetus of people, everyone, then, until it reaches a point that they have changed into well versed dolphins of types: harmonious, vocal and vibrant.

That is the path: *Marxism, then Socialism, and, finally, Communism!*

I'll stop there!

Happiness givers, or happiness feelers?

(ARTICLE 3)

Vedana is the terms used in Buddhism for mind resting or focussed on the aspect of feeling near the chest or the body. Some people feel greater happiness internally than others, but do they give? Sometimes we can feel more "merry" when reaching out to others even if we are not that happy within which is great and can raise the spirits.

The end of the universe, if leading scholars, particularly in the east, are correct is saintly souls who offer a better kind of happier feel by giving not receiving like many do today - though if everyone gives then all receive as well!

If we are just happy in feel, Paula Right continues, then whenever something bad knocks we get tempered and go down, depressed and worry full – it hurts. The late Ajahn Chah, the Thai Buddhist monk from Theravada Buddhism, warrants this by saying that emotions do not last, not even love, they change. But Right goes a step further, saying that it not only wanes within, but the cause is mostly from outside. Wow!

The day will come when all are givers, Right insists, a slight from traditional Buddhism which focuses on internal happiness, mostly not all. "The shift from internal happiness," Right, a leading Buddhist practitioner, focuses on, "is coming". When all are like saints, we will be "Happiness Givers" not receivers, mainly, she adds.

Then, there will be no interference to our happy intake like it is now when everyone agrees, socially, that we are better off bringing happiness to others rather than just instilling it inside.

Right's views, here, are a far stretch from ongoing Buddhism, true. But not far-fetched. For one, Buddhists also accommodate these truths however do not pertinently see that it is the leading difference between the result and the cause. It is, she says, by giving we make others happier not solely by being happy within, always, even if true we should not be hell-bent.

But, the reverse *is* the case. If we are happy within but don't have the value-laden tendency to give no one is happy except yourself and that is selfish, she adds.

This is the reason for EXCHANG VALUE happiness by the give-and-take mechanism and USE VALUE happiness held internal which we can only make usage of.

See?!

Buddhism, Value & Health

(ARTICLE 4)

With You-Valuism, for selflessness, we can be happier because you have to surpass a capitalist mind-frame, which can be ill, with selfishness, until our mental health stabilises.

Remember our value guide!

1. Anything Goes - Fascism
2. Me-Value - Capitalism
3. Us-Value - Socialism, therefore co-operative
4. You-Value - You-Valuism, for selflessness

As it stands, you have to get beyond the me-value tip on the scale, so then you are negative-value-free within the mind, which means, after that, you can have me-value personal goals, at a whim, without being mentally ill!

That's being mentally-free, because it happens automatically since it is a state lower than your normal operating faculty, which is then healthier and can be easily transcended to from the dip.

This is the difference between personal values taught in mental health clinics, and transcendental values outlined here. Both work, if done the correct way!

This was the explanation given by Paula Right at every opportunity to people she worked with in mental health as the reason for so many ill-willed people in modern society, and it stands today, here, in graphic form upright.

She says that You-Valuism is not just for politics. It makes a pertinent point: If we stick to selfish drives and violent behaviour thereof due to the encouragement of capitalism for self-profiteering actions ongoing we will suffer as a result – harshly!

Traditional psychotherapy asks: What do you value? Not explaining what values exist in society and the world at present and how you can, or more precisely, "must" incorporate them into daily life with added vigour. This is the difference between subjectivity and objectivity because we have to know the objective world first and foremost if we want to win. Subjectification, here, subsidises.

"Going into a solipsist world of total subjectivity is dangerous and so too is living externally all the time," Right explains. She adds: "It is a Marxist-led dialectic between theory and practise which is the right balance, even with health, and the value system I've spoken for makes external facts necessary, not sole".

One Marxist snippet on externally-related health online is essential. It says:

"The orientation of this approach as applied within medical sociology is towards the social [or is it economic?] origins of disease. Health outcomes for the population are seen as being influenced by the operation of the capitalist economic system at two levels………First, at the level of the production process itself, health is affected either directly in terms of industrial diseases and injuries, stress-related ill health, or indirectly through the wider effects of the process of commodity production within modern societies. The production processes produce environmental pollution, whilst the process of consuming the commodities themselves have long-term health consequences such as eating processed foods, chemical additives…and so on….."

By saying that "chemical additives" whether in food or not, and the like, is dangerous, as well as exterior, we have to ask why it exists. Is it the value system of the perpetrator? Or something more. Or, is Buddhism more accurate: They are governed by delusion, greed and/or hatred – the three "poisons" – in the religion. Or, more rightly, a mixture of both – rare or common?

This is how Buddhism meets Marxism, not is opposed to it!

And why Buddhists should pick it closely as well like some do!

Because both interiority and exteriority combine here!

Buddhists inside and Marxists outer!

So dare, even in tandem with your own abidings!

Rare!

Everything that arises, re-arises!

(ARTICLE 5)

The famous Buddhist canon is that "everything that arises ceases" it is, so does it? Eventually, yes, but not always! Paula Right explains!

We'd like to "let it pass" when anything incorrect happens to us, but when it reoccurs, we're baffled. We have to see that when people have a strong desire of greed, they keep returning, so it "rearises" so beware. You know they are on a catch for something more or nasty: money, out of envy, spiked or strange!

In one case, a boy did a work placement which was a set up and everyone involved was a capitalist unprincipled so they kept on returning to him for later money on an undisguised know: That he was too feeble to respond when attacked to death! That they thought. He eventually won the war, but it was a battle.

In another, people in a neighbourhood shop were capitalists, again, and he was a Socialist, so both were at equal odds. He won acclaim and they lost the war of words as a result! Their reaction was to poison him through products in the store, food-supplies, where he went regularly. They even attacked his father in the same way, making him fat and dishevelled with poisons and water over-supply recommendations, even poisoning his alcohol bottles. He lived nearby and the local shops were in collusion.

So this went on for many months until they thought he and his son were finished but one Buddhist monk said to one of them that this was happening so the two started taking remedial action without much help from their doctors surgeries. Paula witnessed. And some improvements have been made.

But the case points to this: There seems to be or can, more than one type of capitalist-based domestic war: PRICE WARS are of one kind, now two, and that is PRODUCT WARS as well, unheard of the in the media, which poisons are a part of: True, or false or just maybe?, Paula/Ms. Right asks! Probably not, or is it?

Worse still, it seems the former is not a product of mere upping the prices for profit based on supply and demand, but hijacked, internally, by greed and jealousy, which causes shop sellers and big business to alter the price. This kind of "personal vengeance" can even be seen in doctors surgeries and hospitals where decisioning is made on personal whims rather than professional decisioning.

Paula states: "I've had personal experience once in a GP where a receptionist wanted to know me so well whoever I was and regardless of whether she was nice, so much so that she didn't give me an appointment nearby but made it months away, quite common".

Buddhists know that it is feebler to let suffering into your work from home when unrequired or unwanted but it seems a hard thing to justify to people who are hellish enough to let it do wrong in employment times. Sad, Right goes on.

The famous Buddhist adage whips: "If someone shoots an arrow at you, the first thing to do is pull it out, not ask who shot it" – the cause. So, Paula infatuates, don't blame people especially when working, it's bad conduct. We have to let all aside and do the job right. Just smile, and get out of the mental system that's causing willow when right. That will keep! Then you can make decisions fairly.

Doing things that suit others

(ARTICLE 6)

There was a case in point. A young boy was made to do things "nicely" for his father because it was a hard task and they didn't want his bewilderment, only their betterment, not his – sadly!

It knocked him off guard and made him fragile. Paula notices: "When you give people responsibility, you cannot just think of yourself. You have to bear in mind other's standards, right? So remember, you have to give in to yourself, and put others first. They have to survive also," she said. Not always, but mainly, at the right time, especially!

But you can't, in those situations, always say what you'd like so you have to "differ" to keep the peace. But the "identity", in our former example, with, then, our parents or children and, I might add, brothers and sisters, family, friends and others, remains. This is "difference and identity", the reverse of what Hegel said which was identity and difference - the other way around.

People differ in this way, when there is danger, but not, I prefer, always, when there is a goal to reach with dear ones like peace in a native country for instance when, again, we have to have a "Universal Spirit" – shared, which is another one of Mr. Hegel's adages.

Not many people know this, social, and there is even "difference" when there is no one at odds which makes for life's worry and turbulence which we must overcome, the prestigious writer said. When people share targets, not merit, then everyone wins. We need similar outcomes, for harmony. And that's what Buddhism suits best!

Ms. Right insisted that this is where Marxism and Buddhism never clash if the Buddhist take is for non-tension and the Marxist tip is "The targetter" similar to "Tathataga" in Buddhism, which is defined online as: *an honorific title of a Buddha, especially the Buddha Gautama, or a person who has attained perfection by following*

> *Buddhist principles*, is it right, do they (The Buddhas who achieve this) <u>*target*</u> it?

So target other's well-being as well as your own, have identity & non-difference when all is universally peaceful and target shared or similar goals toward sainthood: the givers of happiness to others for their betterment!

Let's end short!

The Deathless/Timeless conundrum

(ARTICLE 7)

Some say that people never win because they have no time so they envisage a Timeless scenario where people are free, but is this the correct reason for The Timeless puzzle in the Buddhist tradition?

Similarly, many Buddhists believe that the end of existence is the purpose of The Deathless, a situation when because life has ended, there is, then, no need to fear suffering and death for evermore!

Wrong, perhaps, I see, said Paula Right of the editorship once of a leading Asian-geared national paper for South Asia's brown community some years back now – defiantly!

Ms. Right said that "there is no reason that these ideas are worthy in the literal sense even though many should be forgiven for making what could be a mistake without any hesitation at all. Of this I am certain."

"There is something deeper which should be seen not just acknowledge which must I feel put both categories in the proper place I see and envisage."

"The Timeless means that we are in a kind of prison not of our own making which we call this universe which is locked in with a law of Karma to make us merrier at least eventually. It is, therefore, a kind of TIME, prison-like, that we are doing, many of us, not all."

"When we escape from this either way, through added freedom, or by being of service to this very Earth, even creating a Heaven here new and bright, then we are free or at least freer, and we have escaped the prison-worsening feel of TIME. Which is, then, The Timeless."

"Likewise, death can come to us by murder or by ending life or time is up, it has run out, our life energy has ended, all this accounts for or means, literally, DEATH! If we escape this through better health and safety and so reaching a situation where we 'don't die' but live on, fairly, I might add, then this to 'not die' which means we get 'less of death' rendering The Deathless term appropriate."

So, both The Timeless & The Deathless, in Buddhist terms, says Paula, is to say we get 'less' of each until it evaporates or dissolves to empty so what we are left with is the reverse. Hence, the terms resonate meanings to mean precisely this. Nothing else.

"It is ok," Paula adds, "that most not all maybe, strands of Buddhism, have overlooked this for centuries, but that is ok, they might be wrong, or I may be faulty, but this at least makes more common sense that pre-often usages which seem bare and desolate if I am honest".

Let's end now!

Are we on planet Neptune?

(ARTICLE 8)

The name of our planet was exchanged by criminals and we are really living on planet Neptune and Earth is truly what we now call Neptune, the names have been turned around by deviants!

This is what Paula Right remarked today after witnessing something brief: The Earth was named for being sea-life which had to learn to come on land and breath fairly, hence the tag Earth!

After searching the planetary map, near, following the insight in meditation, she learned that it was indeed true – Neptune was all sea which meant the Karma-Rupa (name-form) meaning of Earth was visually right, the life there was beginning to realise that no one was land-based mammal! What a shock!

"I asked the question again and again. Is this why sea-levels are rising? And it occurred to me that it could be. People were living the lie of Earth as their song of life, harshly sometimes, so our planet really was turning into a sea-borne one like Neptune named wrong. Have a look yourself at the pictures of both: Earth and Neptune - to see the sea life there unwitnessed, perhaps, except by top secret agents for government maybe," Paula asks.

The karma-positioning of Neptune maybe to sing the tune of a New Economic Policy (N.E.P) – harmonious – hence N.E.P.....Tune! So, if correct, we may all be living to learn this kind of chorus-led behaviour like wonderful dolphins acting in sync.

The first stage is Socialism, when the politics of the economy, world-wide, is co-operative so stable, unheard of in Earthly, now Neptonian, if true, history. Is this our learning curve? So get prepared, we have to win, says Ms. Right, abruptly!

So, let's do it!

Dialectical Materialism Revisited

(ARTICLE 9)

The need for a dialectical method is not always self-evident and sometimes Buddhists see it as disadvantaged, perhaps rightly if you're superior in mentality with compassion, generosity and kindness at your disposal.

Paula added: "Not many people know what dialectical materialism is and it has been interpreted in diverse fashions, leaving people bemused and often forgetful as to when it is relevant, needed and unsolemn."

Many people interpret DM (Dialectical Materialism or History (DH)) as a conflict between theory and practise, like touched on earlier, but it is not just that. Others see it as optioning, whereas most people see it as the interplay of history. A bit of truth in all, but not only.

Paula said: "Dialectical Materialism is the thought patterning of many people which can see history within their minds, not just on paper. It is the way their minds work. How it came about is a mystery. But I say it comes from analysing peoples' historical past in person to either attack or gain, so nature has given people that capability."

Others see dialectics in a positive light where we can know others' historical dealing and then help steer history itself in a positive direction, which is more religious, known, by some authors, as "Positive Dialectics" with the word metaphysics thrown in for the God connection.

The good thing about Dialectics in mental ability is that you can know history, however far, and therefore, if you gather kindness, then you are more willing to reject it – good!, if all it is, is conflict and wars

One final word. If there is a value-system between peoples; from right or ok to bad, then Dialectical Materialism can be seen as a way of having "mutual reciprocity", a symbiosis, between groups, until equality materialises, a kind of graphic equalizer effect to Sainthood for all now eventually!

So let's leave it there!

Racism history overturned

(ARTICLE 10)

History is replete with instances of racism and social phenomena with a racist slant – cruel!

Paula Right said this is changing!

The editor in chief, once, acknowledged that both the UK police and white-western Sangha are among the top of the league in western society for eradicating racism at the fore, in one country, Britain, first, not always, and it must continue, she sees.

The police in the West must maintain independence in these trying times, with or without a balance of power syndrome, she added. "The police hold responsibility and large-power compared to us, so they bear the burden of protecting all," she went on.

"And they have done it before," she added.

The indigenous Sangha in these countries – European – also regularly get on by with "foreigners" and serve them kindly, humbly and gratefully day in day out so we must commend them, Paula smiles.

"The rest of society must follow".

It is no surprise why I pick these two as non-racist potentially, Paula exclaims. The police are obliged, and can, help people of any colour, like the Sangha here – white. Ajahn Brahm and his team, even in Australia, take time to fly to places like Singapore, Malaysia etc where there are diverse religions, even speaking kindly to Muslims sometimes. They are on the right side of Karma, now at least, god knows when they were young, respectfully, Paula yells.

Buddha's quote says, and they must follow, Paula wallows, that there is no distinction in the sky and they must make the same judgement in life even if different colour groups have to equalise one day – finally!

Even west-type Ajahn Sumedho, the well-known Buddhist monk at Amaravati Buddhist Monastery in Hemel Hempstead, Hertfordshire, UK, was trained by a Thai monk already presented here in this book, Ajahn Chah, Paula recalls.

"There must come a time when all races are one, fair and just and it will happen, first as Socialism comes to the fore. It is not that long away even if some people, like Bob Marley sung, he said that one or two have to or will be discredited for their own good and safety for better on for everybody."

Still, now back to the point, Sumedho, again, regularly has visitors, or did, he is currently retired, who came from Thailand and Sri Lanka mainly with a few white-faces which were the minority, which shows people like him and their monks there at the temple can stand out of the crowd and greet people from other shores gratefully and lovingly, Paula asks.

"And the tradition continues."

It is well documented that migration, not colonialism, has always been a bad temperament for people from host countries who shackle in shoddy accommodation blaming refugees and the like, Paula wallows again.

"But we must win".

The end of capitalism will bring a borderless world once won and then people can live anywhere, but that does not mean that border-type controls will vanish altogether, it is just more kind, where people are not allowed in for other reasons like not enough living space in the region, Paula is pitiful.

"Let's chance it!," she says admiringly.

Reason for reasonable

(ARTICLE 11)

Many people sabotage, spy and fight, which are all symbols of unreasonable behaviour, Paula Right has said. Which must change!

The universities keep spelling out that "we must be reasonable" hence all the acidic attacks on irrationality and non-verbal behaviour, because we should "speak" not "attack" which is the reason for "the speech" in politics, I assume, so keep it up, she continued.

How can we be in such an inflatable, egotistic world with wars and savagery if not for savage behaviour, not upright, the leading journalist went on. This must end soon!

"The Age Of Reason was for some, the enlightened few, but now we need wider scope, so spread your wings and fly," was her message to the world today.

People say there is a concerted attack by some with the strategy of making them not rational as a way of sliding them into the mental health system as mentally ill people to bemuse them thereafter, as an unofficial strategy for the simple-minded, Ms Right suspected.

Some Buddhists say that rationality is bad only trusting intuition, but when put it in the context of "being reasonable" it is not so bad, Rights heralded.

Paula Right added: "Irrationality is delusion, one of the three Buddhist poisons: greed, hatred and, yet again, delusion, which can come if we over-try at being rational, but with logic in, proper temperament and kindness, we can sail on happily."

This is not to say that intuition is not superior in some, it is, but we have to be free, so we need rationality as reasonableness in, near and wide, so people everywhere have to develop a sense of proportion, where we give and offer what is right and just for the situation at least, not avoiding it, she bemused.

People say and wonder why the universities put so much emphasis on REASON, and it is for this very purpose, she assesses, the master of writing and journalism, Paula Right, warranted.

Right insists we are trapped in a world of fright and worry only because we act disproportionately to others and people when all we need is humility.

The transition to a better society will make us more kindlier and it will come about when we see that all this profit-hunting is doing us harm and making us unfree, Paula insinuated.

Socialism is a "reasonable" system if we want better and there is no reason why we shouldn't, the ardent follower of world peace prized.

Social consciousness is rising, so we shouldn't fight for it, but the political will should exist engineered by the far left who need not be money-hungry wannabes, but should be 'advisers of excellence' who can bring in Socialism even for the political few to lead fairly, right and strong!

It will come, but we need patience. The Buddhist Sangha, globally, are fully aware of what socialism is and there are Marxists within their ranks like a Dalai Lama, past or present, she witnessed.

They, too, can help in the bid for World Socialism!

Sri Lanka: You-Valuism and the Muslim Question!

(ARTICLE 12)

The conceiver of You-Valuism Benjamin De Silva has said Sri Lanka's Muslim problem with Buddhists can easily be solved within a You-Valuist remit speaking after regular insights into the dilemma on Reuters and the BBC, Paula Right said.

A number of western countries had labelled the Buddhist "army" [others call it that] there as "Fascists" employing some claim an "Anything Goes" attitude to the dilemma of religious factional politics by both groups, she continued.

She says Benjamin De Silva said "You-Valuism is the idea that religion can exist in a secular way within mainly democratic politics or nearby without worry because there is a graded step up the ladder to selflessness a key factor in religion portrayed by its theoretical ideologues by the far east."

He concluded that there must be a clear demarcation between legitimate religious activity and those of divide and rule which gender also plays no role through.

Mr de Silva spoke of a calmer temper when female people hit the streets in political non-in-fighting which makes for a more peaceful kind of politics which can overcome the gender gap.

You-Valuism is the idea that politics must evolve from:

1. Anything Goes – Fascism…..to
2. Me-Value – Capitalism…..to
3. Us-Value – Socialism and co-operation….to finally..
4. You-Value – a politics of Selflessness at end.

A European Union delegation chief in Colombo Tung-Lai Margue had said then quite recently it was crucial there was "no impunity for hate crimes" in Sri Lanka against Muslims and that the perpetrators ought to be swiftly brought to justice.

But it was brutally argued in the UK Guardian that British foreign policy offends Muslims not only because of Tony Blair's pro-American stance on Iraq and the Middle East, but also because of Britain's thorough indifference to crises faced by smaller Muslim populations outside of Europe.

And this in then the past month, as the world focused on Lebanon with a cursory glance at Iraq and Afghanistan and conflicts erupting elsewhere went unnoticed, it says.

Many Muslims and other minority groups in danger like Sri Lankan Tamils did often argue they are indigenous peoples and deserve the respect of the host nation, whether in the US or further afield, with one Muslim author who reports say has published a book titled 'Muslims in America: Seven centuries of History (1312-2000)' arguing the first Muslims came to America 180 years before the European settlers came following Christopher Columbus' voyage in 1492.

Mind evolve unadapting

(ARTICLCE 13)

Be yourself, rather than adapt haphazardly!
These were the words of Paula Right after assessing the survival of the fittest thesis which says the most-feeble perish in nature's bid to hunt the strongest. Wrong, she takes on. What is strong or fit anyway?, she asks.

And if you make people worry about adaptation, the Karmic result is worry yourself – the stress syndrome, she went on, which Buddhism unpermits!

So, do we need a dole service or not, especially for the weak or turbulent, mentally?

"There are many people who starve without being paid pittance. Remember business came from the peasantry, who wanted more money – profit, so if they want the same, they would, perhaps, need not want to work for more, if they so pick, before Socialism arrives, when there will be universal welfare and 'encouragement' to work incentively, and educationally, not forced, like under capitalism."

"Capitalists and business owners need help also, remember we have to be on the ball if we want a truly free society eventually, one that supersedes even Socialism.

When we stress for worrying others, that's the Buddhist remit, in one way.

Another cause is remembrance, Paula adds.

"Many people remember things not good which causes so much worry they get depressed and stubborn even, sometimes. So we need an empty mind, like binary code to 'nothing'".

An article states: 'The Heart Sutra says, "all phenomena in their own-being are empty." It doesn't say "all phenomena are empty." This distinction is vital. "Own-being" means separate independent existence. The passage means that nothing we see or hear (or are) stands alone; everything is a tentative expression of one seamless, ever-changing landscape. So though no individual person or thing has any permanent, fixed identity, everything taken together is what Thich Nhat Hanh calls "interbeing." This term embraces the positive aspect of

emptiness as it is lived and acted by a person of wisdom —
with its sense of connection, compassion and love. Think of the
Dalai Lama himself and the kind of person he is — generous,
humble, smiling and laughing — and we can see that a mere
intellectual reading of emptiness fails to get at its practical
joyous quality in spiritual life. So emptiness has two aspects,
one negative and the other quite positive.'
But Paula is more forthright. She admits we can't be sure of all
necessary meanings of the word or concept of "emptiness" in
Buddhism, but says what we can be sure of is that the mind of
emptiness can be rationally true, not just meaningful, but in a
way, that loses remembrance and is free of intrusive thinking,
an aspect of schizophrenia, and, she ensures, that can be
evolved!
"Even murderers with murderous thoughts can sit in
contemplation and focus on the breath to clear the mind, once
free from others, and "can not talk" – be silent, so the mind
sits stills."
"We have had a look at the history of 'movement' since the big
bang, which means we cannot sit in complete stillness for very
long. so try," she asks. Even industrialisation was heavy and
took its toll unsolemnly.
As Ajahn Brahm, the head monk or abbot of The Buddhist
Society Of Western Australia attests for, solemnity brings
greater depth not meaningfulness, and necessarily, or it can -
But we need more than Socialism as a social force sometimes,
we need space.

'The ending of things' like war

(ARTICLE 14)

Buddhism states to 'notice the ending of things'.

Kung Fu says to 'stop'. Let's not explain, Paula warrants.

My father, and former Sri Lanka Television, chairman, Vasantha-Raja, was not a Kung Fu expert but a Buddhist-leaning theoretician, even political, and wanted "the _end_ of war everywhere, Paula explains.

That is why he said that even separatist movements can be curtailed and defeated theoretically by aligning them with 'word-peace-vision' where separate states can re-align regionally into South Asian and so Socialist blocks which are war-free! See it?

If people are so divided they can sidestep total isolation and become part of a one world federal socialist block vision encompassing every old and new country – even separatism itself can be overcome.

That's the idea – and true – not tacky - as some jealous spokespeople classified him!

Paula added: "If we focus on the end of wars and other evils we will eventually stop them also like the best Kung Fu masters want true or as well."

That's the Buddhist rook to the ending of things thesis.

Not on the "re-alignment" of things like wars!

"Some analysis given to the police say that leading philosophy rooks might be unconsciously behind the _navigation_ for realignment of things like war, which makes them hell-bent badly, but that can be overcome internally and mentally with the proper not just normal use of Buddhism to The Deathless, everlasting life when we overcome _all_ or _most_ health problems and similar things well or properly!

So let's prosper with the 'ending of things' thesis and make world peace our goal like my dadda Vasantha-Raja did, alias.

After all the war-to-peace dialectic is a very different kind of one from the ordinary conflictual type because, here the former dissolves the latter – a more Buddhist focus, on the

"ending", not a dismantling worry like normal dialectics held wrongly!
I end!

TASTE OR WAR?

(ARTICLE 15)

The western philosophical tradition which, in the progressive field, focuses on "class" is not enough to divert the bad taste of conflict and antagonism which grips the world today. We need a "taste" philosophy! And Buddhism is it!

'The Way It Is,' means the tastefulness of things, and that's right!

We suffer terrible problems when we just act without thinking about it, Ms Right went on. We have to be tasteful all the time and notice the tasteless things people do so we can improve earnestly.

And that means sharing happiness as well not just having it within as said before, so recommend it to others also so we have an exchange mechanism in place for happiness not just a use one where we make usage of our inner strength for our own selfish rewards or stealing it from others by using them for our own benefit – manipulation and the user syndrome.

Now that's tasteful. And so is sharing knowledge, advise, tips etc for others peoples' well-being not just our own even if the conditions are not apt, financially, for everyone across the globe now truly yet.

Because it will when You-Valuism, based on Buddhism, hits the mark and renders everyone selfless at some stage in a way that triumphs because being selfless is an exchange function not an internal one so do it and see the difference – steady!

Buddha always said "Be Selfless" and that's what distinguishes the region it is from, but Buddhism is for all continents, still we need confidence that giving "happiness to others" is as powerful or more so than "just" happiness within.

That's my contribution, Ms. Right signified.

There are many people who a happier within who do not have the taste or foresight to give it to other people unsolemnly because they are too selfish so that must stop and can because it is an evolve – be there!

And foresight is where it's at. Buddha also says 'mind is the forerunner of all things' and that must be right so this means it can see in advance so train therein if necessary at least once in a while until through!

But taste is more important, maybe, maybe not! So, what is it, not defined online easily. In this context it means "seeing the worth of things - in their texture as they are…kind or ugly…good or bad, also opting for what is better. Always seeing what's artistic and worthwhile in situations and things" [my definition]. Now that's tasteful.

But war isn't. Or maybe I should say '"So"….war isn't', because war certainly isn't worthwhile *if* there are options even if we have to train to improve ourselves to act more virtuously to get there unsternly.

So, let's phase in to something far better, which is You-Valuism itself. All South Asian religions merge on selflessness now so that particular region is special, openly attesting to Rebirth & Karma first I think, says Paula, so let's pay it due respects and encourage others to follow: kindly, happily and generously – with TASTE!

YOU-VALUISM UNHARSH

(ARTICLE 16)

Buddhists say that business and virtue meet in generosity!
Well, does it?

We say that this generousness is in "product design"; the more
generous the more benefit it brings to the consumer so more
priceless.

Hence the effort in multi-media design where mobiles, email,
cameras, computers exist as one, in the same gadget now.

Now, this generous mind-frame can be brought to life!

With You-Valuism, it exists as a subset, inferior to religiously-
motivated selflessness, but not far from it – generous true!

Paula states: "We need more happier social relations not just
in products and design but in persona in what we do and how
we react and business has a head start, not always, but
sometimes, and workers can follow, because they are needed,
in some situations, even more than business, but not always for
them, not us, because we treasure everyone who brings worth
to others even unconsciously!"

This means that You-Valuism, selflessness in the economy, is
right for business-people not just everybody, because Marx
said that political economy is the politics of the economy, and if
it's a selfless one, then that suffices to make everyone happier
and it can sooner rather than late."

The battle is on!

Can Conservatives in Britain or the Labour party here win
You-Valuism primarily and first, who will win?

The stakes are on!

Paula advises both main UK parties: "The social phenomena
of Phenomenology of Spirit of You-Valuism – like Hegel's - is
on, even on TV, news and outer it, but remember," she
reminds, "not to find meaning truthfully, and believe in that,
but instead find truth in meaning…unlike the Existential
philosophy which sees life as meaningless first then adds
meaning, not truth, on. Get it right," she warrants.

The path to You-Valuism is for business also, she tells
Conservatives, which means we should stop upping the prices

because of avenge, conversely, rather than on, properly, supply and demand, she adds.

That is what *Das Kapital* (Karl Marx) is about, even as co-operatively for him, selfless for us, she, again, says – politely. This kind of emotional entanglement when bought into business, instead of co-operation or selflessness in supply-demand relations is counter-productive and leads to misery. Even nature is devoid of uncontrolled emotive worry and acts deliberately, Paula Right warned the Conservatives and Labour, adding that her journalistic and experimental investigation into Earth-life for everyone discovered that nature might be conscious for real, even experimenting with sound by wind and water and knocking on tables which found that it seems to have consciousness and can even utter words! In one such experiment, Paula found that water was, when heard with high-focus like meditation, even speaking and said things like in pre-feudal Britain and globally, pre-peasantry life and folk we self-destructive and suicidal after prolonged failure, overall, in bitter war – really, she exclaimed!

Similar incidents happen today!

We have to end it!

War, I mean and emotive jealousy and bitterness and anger, which bring it and other similar events to "no life"!

So work with it, until we win!

Let's end here!

BEFORE THE BIG BANG NOW!

(ARTICLE 17)

Richard Dawkins said there is no such thing as a God. But Hindus say there are millions. God-types can be recognised by their triangular head-shapes seen in numerous people here strong.

Scientists, until now, say we don't know what happened before the big bang, but now there are regular images of the gas-type-beings in images of smoke, not screen, because it is visible, that existed prior. See online. I saw one of these just.

Paul Right said this is obvious: "We were here before the big bang occurred and something brought us in!"

Whether it was a God or a Karma force is unknown. However, recent meditations by Paula, an ardent meditation master, with Divine Eye capabilities, said it could have been Karma-force, even "within" God. Why? Because the meditations with audio Divine Ear also, perhaps, insist that the value-system of the folks that lived then, or maybe there, were "dis-drain" folks, which meant they dismissed draining others for more, a symbol of work where similar things have to happen, where they have to give in Karmaland instead, an aspect of Karma law, looks like!

The other reason for the Karma link, is that, the meditation revealed, on audio as well, that, primarily, these beings, mainly, not all, were gassy folks which killed smaller beings for fear of attack, which was wrong if they were more scared, so Karma brings them in, in this universe, in totality, as substance creatures, with physicality, who need to learn not attacking anyone is right, because since it has physicality, thar means you can be killed in person by other physical objects like knives, guns and bombs, unlikely if you are just gas now – true or false! Maybe! Hope not!

They thought they were safe, and could attack anyone, with poison, the meditation reveals, or maybe suggests, but now they have to survive as substance beings with a body, to stop it – the Karma link again!

So, is this accidental? Like some scientists, not Dawkins, say?

No. If true!
Dawkins insists we have a selfish gene as well, but reality shows that some people are encouraging selflessness, like in South Asian ethno-religious literature, and others, say in China, taught co-operative politics of the economy, in theory or ideally, even if not in practise, fully, yet. So we are near something brighter, which is Socialism itself, if so many people want more, a great improvement to our "dis-drain" origin or start, if true now!

So many people have improved, even though a lot of work needs to be done, with an abundance of inventions, literature and non-phoney people around as well as the odd dodgy bloke, say some, but it is improving either way, however far behind some are, even if in the many, as other groups or spokespeople contend. The truth, in all probability, is somewhere inbetween: a mixture of good and bad say! But it is moving to better, until done!

So get with it!

"POSITIONS" OF WAR

(ARTICLE 18)

The art of war can be precarious! "Ge up, go to work, as a lecturer, do some teaching, go to your office, read a book, and then plan your exit. You kill." Is is the lifestyle of many engaged in battle, hope not, but I say it happens not just in official war-zones, but in every war-pitted, as perceived, even badly, unclear country!

This is what Paula right thought as she walked the towns in major capitals nearly eight years ago. This has happened, she assumes, with evidence not yet conclusive.

Does full-blown conflict erupt like this?, she asks.

Well there is a way out now truly for sure!

And that is co-operation, the politics of it, which at the pinnacle of it is co-operative social relations even within states, already in in one special sense – as service-to-co-operative relates – which everyone is doing uncanny: in shops, supermarkets and galleries! Not, property-relations as such! Only the money values differ in capitalism.

Communism, the latter deal, is "The Truce" where all end-to-war meets. You-Valuism is the freedom where we are no longer self but for others in practise and deed.

Our deeds come from our intentions, Paula Rights insists. So we have to have right intention: for generosity and non-greed. Others are "embedded" dysfunctionally in bad action so it runs deeper, but their way out is similar, Paula says. This is why the Buddhist path, without impediments, starts sometimes, in literature, with Right Intention as the start of the path," Paula unwarrants. So get there!, she says unblindly. The full Buddhist line of defence is: Wisdom, Virtue & Concentration!

There was no wisdom-type proof, how could there be?, for the recent attack and fire in Britain which left several dead in the block of flats which was inspected by some or one before the initially investigated-as-terrorist-incident occurred.

Paula warrants: "There has to be truce, world-wide, now that is wise, where groups and factions realise that there is only one way out, and that is Benjamin De Silva's path for politics which starts with Existentialism and no-value and moves up after capitalism and socialism, to selflessness, namely You-Valuism.

Remember, You-Valuism is free and is the true end to the liberation of the polity in service terms, because you are no longer concerned about self but care only for others primary, not just!, Paula says flamboyantly.

All religions say it, but Buddhism expresses it the most, she goes on undefensively!

For that, we should be grateful.

Gratitude is just FORE and then GIVING which translates to "giving in advance" which means you are not burdened by others peoples' maliciousness and greed, you just give on, unlimitedly!

When we reach this state of "Unlimitedness" we can offer things like love and compassion anytime we want, it's just there – forever! So people have it in different virtues, like generosity or kindness, but with forgiveness, we surrender love to ourselves as well and never get washed up again.

Like Ajhan Brahm says, whatever you do, the door of my heart is open to you, which is what his father told him – unlimited compassion for his child!

Let him win!

On a lighter note…Beautiful women and rebirth lineage!

Meditations reveal Rebirth lineages. And for some it is emphatic. Beautiful women, for instance, come from "lemming" strand over Rebirths exemplified by the fact that those animal type, reminiscent in squirrels as well, hold their palms face down in front of them, something many women, especially beautiful ones, do as well, one meditation and philosophical investigation, Earth-wide, revealed. The animal of 'dear' may be another line over Rebirths.
Just a note!

The workers' economy, not state!

(ARTICLE 19)

The way or path to Socialism in each nation state is to get government or the state, primarily, not always, that is, get it to match business shop by shop with free products and services or generally: small businesses, medium and large, even multi-national, until all has to through competition reduce profit to freebie. Then, the workers state would disappear under administration handed over to socialist-business models where everyone is equal: consumer and now then the distributor! Then we'll have a workers' economy, not a workforce state, fair – and true!

This is what Paula Right said to people who dismissed her dream of Socialism when she was little until it ushers in a new era later even Socialism-free to You-Valuism, a selfless economy!

A future repeat here in this book: "Socialism-free" means we have instilled co-operative social ethics so strong in the psyche, it becomes like second hand, unthinking, an aspect of the very idea of freedom in the Buddhist traditional context of the east, not west yet – but soon!

Except for in neurology, but where it falls short is it seems here to be limited to what you do, like occupationally, not on what you enact – like a co-operative lifestyle or selfless one, which it can be, in neurology plainly. Paula smiles.

That about finishes it!

The Earth liberation business plan

(ARTICLE 20)

Philosophy-based people like Kant, Aristotle, Hobbes and Mill all said we need virtue and politics to mx harmoniously and patiently and it does under You-Valuism!

Paula Right added: "Some people are moral in capacity, but haven't achieved virtue fully, which means galliant - the ideal pinnacle of the saint, hero or knight, a turbulent episode when horse-riders saved or tried to rescue brutally strung women locked in dungeons or secret towers for love or aura". Not very nice.

The Buddhist definition of nobility is superior and sees own suffering as no barrier to you liberating others to fruition. It can work!

Liberation in politics is yet not complete.

ISHI, or Benjamin De Silva, tried.

The idea is this. Virtue in politics means, finally, selflessness, not co-operation for your own freedom, but giving to others their own freer. That's when it's complete. So, this applies to daily life, because politics is everywhere, not just in the polity! None of the above Political Theorists saw this, Paula states.

The Earth Liberation Business plan is the following path:

1. **Anything Goes – Fascism**
2. **Me-Value – Capitalism**
3. **Us-Value – Socialism and Communism**
4. **You-Value – You Valuism..the politics of selflessness!**

It can win!

When everyone is self-free, not thinking about themselves all the time with "me-time" and the rest, we all get merrier and like each other better, but currently all of us have only reached the ME-VALUE STAGE of capitalism, with odd skirmishes into Fascism from time to time historically untrue.

It was Adam Smith that spoke of the wealth of nations and competitive advantage theory with generosity as the goal for

money and national superiority in the competitive world of global economy – Fine.

It was for the progressive stage to Feudalism, but we need an end to a few things first: global poverty, crime, anything goes values, war, non-augmentation from mistakes and social worry, is Paula's main worry – and only Socialism can win – Next!

Marx said primitive Socialism came first which even exists as co-operative seeds in peasant-life, not very strong though I assume. But tribal life earlier was a worry beyond belief even if it had to look after only a few.

Paula says the technology syndrome in Marx means this, Why should people go without the most modern technology based on supply and demand at full, not yet ideal, when there is an abundance of it free under Socialism.

So, lets' win!

But Hobbes thought we couldn't, without a world sovereign. He said there was a state of nature too strong in animal and human life that nothing weak could work, and China followed with Marx. Well, under You-Valuism there is no need for a ruler of any kind, because when people hit this last stage of politics globally and beyond on Earth further than your own man, perhaps, also, proper, and workable, there will be no need for the state; the Magic Zero in Benjamin De Silva's work, where the "no state" position after it exists, not before, is superior without it even as empty of it! Baffled? You should be, because that's a "Higher Zero", not the centre spot of the mathematical system, it is unheard of life-wide here so far, Paula assumes.

So, let's get there soon!

Kant in political theory

(ARTICLE 21)

Many people criticised Paula Right for studying philosophy, even as a drop-out. But she withstood, carrying on even out of school with a special favourite for Kant, the German PE instructor (philosophy educator) - then!

But now she revels in how Kant likened wealth-pursuers, non-military, to Moles in the animal Kingdom and philosophers to heavenly beings however down-trodden and docile.

"We knew it was right in a war climate even in Britain where racism is high, even as covert mainly, with positions as "the lawyer", "the hairdresser" and "the postman" filled with military-type personalities - hidden, widespread and unstrong - in some countries!

Without military, Kant's perfect fit Karma theory was unknown in his writing, but he acted like a Buddhist, speaking of the "perpetual peace" that philosophers wanted which we now know can only come through co-operative states and people within a Socialist remit!

Marx's heralding!

Marx and Kant knew of the difference between Theory & Practise and what it meant for the perfect state which was geared towards progress and moral virtue – which has been covered.

But rooks in the modern era use it covertly, to say you have to understand reality for your theory to be right, and if it backfires in practice, in the real world, then its wrong theory, a stunt for more like in business.

The guise is, Paula warns,…is to instill, forcefully, those peoples' or victim's say downfall after the advice, so as to make it seem that they are weak, and thereby wrong theoretically, and then make them dependant as a result on them for prior knowledge, the wrong use if any of Dependency Theory in so-called "Third World" not "Value" studies, done mainly for _salli_ (money in Sri Lanka) and humiliation purposes!

But Kant spoke of the Theory/Practice dilemma in abundance differently, more prime, saying that it ought to be applied in three areas for improvement primarily: in morality, politics and for mankind!

Paula Right used it herein for number two, for politics, first, but other scopes later followed frankly, and she did it, I say, following in the footsteps of Benjamin De Silva, or ISHI for short, the journalist and inventor of You-Valuism itself!

You-Valuism, unlike Kant, says be selfless, I repeat, again, frankly, now, but you can't be happy with selflessness alone, you have to give happy feeling to others by being generous, kind and compassionate always, Paula repeats.

In common usage, Paula adds, people say just "be happy" but that is wrong because simply being happy doesn't mean you exchange it and give it to others and in the reverse way from others to you as well now.

But, when you do, that's proper selflessness and it always comes back if everyone is doing it so we must get to that point quickly – without reverse, Paula laughs.

And it is funny. Because Buddhists have always maintained the importance of happiness within, but I contend that this is no guarantee that it will be shared, or better, again, exchanged like a candle that gives so many other ones a flame when they are lit by it.

Now the time is right to unexplain, Paula sighs.

How widespread are the Powers in Buddhism?

(ARTICLE 22)

Some analysts say only a few people have powers in Buddhism, but Paula says they are popular and in disbelief, she interprets using Buddhist scripture, applied to the modern!

The truth is anyone can have power, maybe not the Form or Idea of it, Perfect and Universal however if it exists strong as Movement powers, then why, if not for Buddhism itself?

So how do you justify it? I say, don't!

Paula continues: "I experienced brown or Asian people in Britain being attacked by Asians themselves while white-westerners like myself were being kind non-abrupt, so is this a trick using the power of change, changing skin colour, a power not revealed in Buddhism, by a group of whites or blacks even or a mix to do it where white or blacks, even Oriental, change into South Asian brown to deceive like this?", otherwise why does it happen, if you're the same skin colour unracist as well? Not perfecto!

The goal, perhaps: To make people side with the West, if white, I think now and make them hate their own kind when real South Asians are selfless in potency or potential at least, a strategy by maybe some westerners maybe of war-mindedness ones, even if not overt! Wrong, it misfired, if true, because Asians in the South are all unified now by a political philosophy which hits the peak – You-Valuism itself!

The idea in another rook, it seems, similar to Buddhist stories in the scriptures, was to make it seem that Asian women didn't like one brown-Asian man so he goes to white-Western females forcefully instead of voluntarily, mutually, with the aim of stealing his wealth once he provides for her, because he was initially seen as wealthy by all!, I assume, says Paula now.

Sorry to bang on about stealing throughout this book, Paula adds.

"But it is necessary......"

Power for wealth or any covert operation doesn't work in Karmaland and shouldn't, Paula warrants.

"For obvious reasons now!"

Any peoples on earth, even the harshest, if one, can have power, Paula warns. And it is dangerous if we are not kind, not just not good.

So, let's stop it, soon when in power with You-Valuism of selflessness and non-greed.

Go for it – strong, proportionally and gradually!, Paula stumbles.

"The racist nature of war has to stop, even without powers in,....something Bob Marley yelled about!"

So stop it, the powering, too far, or wrong in, is what The Buddha cautioned us of!!!

A DIVERSION!

(ARTICLE 23)

Some have yelled at me for not assuring them that racism will end in relationships between skin types: Black, White, Oriental & Brown, Paula yells.

The black-white relationship, mixed, is more common than white with other races. Wow!, Paula exclaims.

She explains. The value system in white and black is similar but Orientals and browns have diverged except for Christianity and philosophy in the West - under capitalism. The Anything Goes unhappy for success and me-value individualism of the capitalist drive is similar where they blend in black and white.

But Oriental and Brown try at best to be more progressive with the family system, co-operative at ideal, not always in practise, and South Asia's religion say selflessness is even higher, which they correspond to – firmly, again, not always in action, but they try.

Even Oriental religion, of the selfless type, is firmly not only mostly, South Asian at start, I see.

They will all blend when our politics of selflessness, again, reaches the peak in all cultures.

Then, we will see more of a mix with others skins and the west as true!

You have to be true really in this life which is the avoidance of death and violence as its goal, and to be happy, not just happiness within but shared we have to give to each other, and it will come eventually.

Not now, but soon, when all is equal and fair, a day on the rise. Be there!

Overcoming poor looks helps, for all, and in Karma world that is done over Rebirth by being moral everywhere in with everyone!

Moorishism

(ARTICLE 24)

Moorism, or the latter, Moorishism, my invention, Paula smiles, is wanting MORE superstitiously unwavering and ruthlessly by exhausting others until hell-bent either way for completion, a business mentality like for money gone wrong for yourself as well even unknowingly and it happens – sadly, by bashing similar or unsimilar types for it strong in your own eyes but not in truth under Karma law! And it is carried out even violently to others by many people without considering the repercussions, Paula wins for herself and you. Even the media and people within it have done it regularly, Paula looks grim she said, and it can change, easily though! It is the undertone of business when greed is strong even for things other than money! But rooks bring it into personal life as well. Be self-conscious of it and shift safely if it occurs to you strongly in personality or actioning.

Moorish types get, I assume, pushed or go themselves into business for that is where you get more of things, also like in a consumer economy designed by businesses where all you want is more products – sad!

Another strategy of Moorists is to attack with products or threaten to kill someone superior often, not always, depending on integrity, so that they force an "association" with you until you befriend THEM, not the other way round often, to rook prestige, like in "associative marketing" but between people for their benefit, a trait which may go back to ancient history even before the big bang, Paula states boldly, we must overcome.

Let's stop, Paula says abruptly.

She then carries on!

Moorish people may stop you doing things for yourself by creating laziness in you, things done not selfishly but happily, so don't want you to be this way. They can even disrupt or secretly enter you're your social life, sometimes leaving you isolated for a gambit.

Another trick is doing similar things to you like entering your politics to, again, create association, unsurely though and deceptively, for a rook for more from you, like with business.

Another strategy by the Moorists is to secretly do work for you behind your back and later gain from you for the service, a kind of Relationship Marketing where we are then linked forcefully!

If gone wrong, they then attack people close to you for the failure! Or try another way by getting you to help others known to them instead. Another cause of action is not getting MORE from you but the MOST from you – Mostlyists then.

Back to Moorism. One rook even took money from a publishing company that one person was associated with, they had a prior relationship to them and gambled on a connivance to steal his book money who she had no rights to – for, again, MORE!

Even some media personnel can, experimentally, want MORE from some people therein by associating an individual with "terrible things" that they are not associated with really to cause a stir and compel them for MORE! Money, knowledge, guidance.

Another Moorish strategy is digging into and reducing the "pride" of people, mainly leaders, and trying to reduce it in advance before asking for gain.

Others want "AS MUCH AS THEY CAN", not MORE or MOST!!

Want BETTER, not more or most or much is the advice!, Paula smiles!

YOU-VLAUISM: An art or a science?

(ARTICLE 25)

You-Valuism is *Avant-Garde* as an art!

The definition of Avant-Garde online is: "New and experimental ideas and methods in art, music, or literature".

You-Valuism is new and is a "fore-guard" as in French meaning!

But it is also a science as people can "cause" it to materialise in linear after Socialism, for a politics of selfless behaviour in the polity and across nations.

Paula states: "You-Valuism was made up in a rational way but no one has ever thought of a politics above Socialism, it has always been seen as the highest point of political development with Communism at the top or peak or pinnacle now."

But soon the highest point of political development will be a selfless ethos!

Some commentators say Socialism globally and must also therefore be You-Valuism world-wide will never reach its mark of acceptance, but it will, not inevitably, but really when people "accept" lower at this point with a run for higher later.

This is the worry! People do not want to win unblind with heartfelt feelings for themselves and self-forgiveness, you have to give to you self, advancely and without condition.

Those who have more wisdom will rest peacefully and acknowledge they are still not co-operative, then the new will materialise unflamboyantly in time, well.

Same for selfless.

Paula assumes: "The reason for conflict when all is clear politically is no acceptance for what is right and true, that's all we need - frank. This accepting ourselves and the world around us, even in politics, structurally correct, is a central hygiene of Buddhism, and we should be clean, with us - and YOU."

"Because You-Valuism reaches the heights of cleanliness where common crime will disappear and those around us will not have to live in fear when it is near."

So stay out of trouble, and get artistic!

SNIPPET

Our world of landmasses should be re-named as one country because the word world means precisely that the regions within it are divided, hence the phrase "One World" to rectify this, especially within the human sphere. By re-calling the world a country this will act as a catalyst in helping to prevent any further divisive stages far better than leaving it as one world futurebound, even with one army present soon to assist! Its name could be "Zarco" which is intended to mean "No worry" as a joke because worrying others through war, conflict and arguments is what has caused the stress within the minds of many for oneself and others if they rebound unwillingly and has thereby brought in the no-stress religion of Buddhism so far.

EXISTENCE OR "LIFEENCE"?

(ARTICLE 26)

We normally call life existence, but existence, if we name it that, is for living and being alive like the trees, animals and even clouds/sky – great. This is why it is really "Lifeence" not "existence", again, because once things live instead of just exist which is what existence is for, then they are alive, and when people are alive – there is, now, LIFE, not LIVE anymore, so the idea, strong, is for lifeness in our hearts and sights and experience, so our environment is for LIFEENCE itself not existence finally!

This where we are heading!

Not as the hustle and bustle of life for hustling and baffling but non-hustle and non-baffle which is better and higher so get there true!

This is what Paula Right, says, remarkably.

This is the "context" of life, beauty not existing, but we still have to have the desire to become saintly souls like Ayurveda and/or Hinduism implies, something Vasantha-Raja, my father, continually says and teaches in his philosophical work as a master of Philosophy from a top London University.

And Buddhism says it. The value-system of Buddhism is – Compassion, not co-operation, first, not only, which is what the saint-soul or non-soul version of Buddhism warns, if not all of us can see past lives with thought, as some, only through meditation like in South Asia now. Which takes off the burden. To No-Soul, then, if you can't remember!

Paula is frank: "This is the basis of Lifeence. To see the aliveness in life, including us, if we all get there. What a wonderful world. And Universe. Let's win. Win it. Imagine what it would be if Compassion is installed in everything and everyone as well, a Buddhist world, not binary to zero coding for non-evil once we get to it."

So, remember, life is to witness that aliveness in all, so stop existing Existentialists and live, so we can see the beauty in you and everyone.

In a military dilemma, it's different. So let's end world war,
otherwise we have to "think" more not go empty to survive, so
"I am" that, unwaveringly, for now not always if in.
The phrase "I think therefore I am" warrants it.
That's Sartre!
An existentialist!
True!

Normal to strong

(SNIPPET 2)

The normalisation-base of society and mankind should be co-operative, not alone, but as a stable, to beat the selfish drive and crime – fair! Then everyone is equal! Marxism, the "targeting" of it, can get us there sooner than either Socialism, political, or Communism – which is "Accomplishment" of it soon. We don't have to detour, but can, but don't make it abnormal at start, hence co-operation, the next stage in history, the targetter will help! Stopping more divergent behaviour is essential for mental health, and, if so, crime will end. Be strong, Paula warrants, it is wise! "The foundation is not it because that can break, it is more of a base, because this is certainly more sure. With co-operation as the base, then, we can generate freely for more diverse not divergent, sour, behaviour, which can "normalise" people greatly and in general as a cross-sectional whole – for steadier harmonious freedom: the next country not world now, system, fine! A country-system to subdue the world-system concept finally."

Marx & Buddha

(ARTICLE 27)

It is normally stated that Marx is a materialist because he is concentrating on reality, well reality can be non-material like ether, Paula Right explains sincerely.

Others say Buddha is mental, but not only, even if most of Buddha-theory is, why?, we may wonder and the answer is this, if we are physically ill, the mind works miracles _neme_ ("not", in Sinhala, the language of the majoritarian Sinhalese in Sri Lanka now, Ceylon before).

So, we must be careful.

There is a dialectic between theory and practise when studying Karl Marx, but in a special way. He read "the book" prior to his own understandings (Theory), then saw reality as different even in behaviour – Capitalism, (Practise), then reverted to his own theorising of reality with higher Enlightenment, namely Socialism (back to Theory and on). Dialectics.

Even I go through it, Paula smiles, yet again.

When at university, I analysed the books in politics, and tried, when near, to see if it corresponded to reality so that I could test where it was true.

Truth is "the point" of academic writing, Paula examines. "Reality" is what's out there.

Buddha saw what was within only _neme_, he saw the body as well, what is "on" us most not just within, and saw it had to be strong and healthy, unlike what some, not all, monks say. If we are upright in "spirit" and violent in body and mind, then that fits the eastern tradition, which says lead with spirit, not heart if it is evil.

So, Buddha was, then, _more_ than a subjectivist.

And Marx is more than a Dialectics man, I see, says Paul Right vehemently.

Marx is primarily an "Experientialist" if what he claims is that once property-relations are scrapped and we include service and co-operation in our dealing with people, then that climate of annexing others with colonialization will end to bring world peace if it is done between nations, regionally and in personal life always and everywhere irreversibly – right?

World peace is an "experience" if it is relational – between us!

196

That is why I say happiness is a relationship between people too – frank!
Not just within, Pauls re-smiles.
So she is happy for one reason only: Both Marx and Buddha wanted the *experience* of world peace to materialise although in different ways, it seems, one psychologically primarily not as the only means with health though – Buddha, and Marx needed a more rational way to overcome the need for greed through practising co-operation unclumsy.
So this is where we should end.
Both are experientialist if what they yearn for is the "result" finally of a world view with no borders and distinctions not only the "journey" that will get us there, something that goes beyond just a path and road, but a frequent attempt to harness our capacity for freedom: kindly, purposefully and happily.
Good!
Now more!

From where you are

(SNIPPET 3)

People often say we can't achieve anything and have to follow, again, a journey or a path – long! But I say different. We can all give now, truly as well, even if we need linear guidance, and that is what the value-systems of Earth are all based on. Some people, religions or regions, give more, much more than others. Some people are still racist though, so largely give to their own kind, especially in confused territories, sadly, but it can change. When we give kindness to other skin-colours then we make others happy, not just each other within a sect – sectional politics. So give freely to more and more so everyone is given happiness eventually, not just contained within, but spread widely!

UNIVERSAL WISDOM

(ARTICLE 28)

'Universal' means within each universe covering all of them. But there is more to lifeence (not existence now) than universal experience, which is time, remember, prisony, everything in a not without a "contained" universe, perhaps, harsh and trappy, how much more is sparse beyond the experience of a universe, even parallel ones?

But it is not wise in universal experience, and value-systems of peoples says it all envisioningly" Paula earmarks.

Paula remarks: We have to get wiser!

All of us.

In this uni-verse as well, "verse" because, now, all of us have to sing together harmoniously the tune of Sainthood – like dolphins do!

Now that's wise.

Paula is.

Like Ajahn Brahm explains, the concept of infinity, as given by one well-known poet, exists, he says, because it resembles the "stupidity" of mankind. And he is right, if all the value-system shows is all we are is selfish at present within capitalist confines, that's wrong as well as mad, what more could there be even within? – foolish really.

If we give more and more, it becomes infinite. Wow. There is no limit to width or scope or other dimensions – strong! This is real, the real strength of the concept of the infinite abode – true as well! Well....

If people like you, for sure, not just to see you close up, which is how some peoples' emotions can work, theoretically, but actually, then they will give you more, but you have to give to contend for friendship now don't you - true?

How big is infinite in this context? Well....

Now that's wise, not stupid, a new view of infinity in the wisdom gallery!

We could really win, when no one has nothing to hide, which they do now if they don't want to take off this selfish straight jacket and improve capacity!

Let's win.
More wisdom! Widespread! By giving! Each of us!
And free with it!

ENCOURAGEMENT TO WEST

(ARTICLE 29)

The west need not worry that the value-system analysis brings it into second place on the world map, after Existentialism and Anything Goes, which can be surpassed, because the value-game has as its purpose "giving more" cross-culturally as well, which is how its designed…looks like. So it, The West, can win – strong!

Business has generosity in it, but Socialism offers more now! Paula is adamant.

"We can have the courage to come from behind even if only in one way, but it is vital. So let's accept lower just for this, and improve. One day Christianity can move from 'giving more than you receive' to 'being selfless' – higher -which renders it similar to the white-western-Muslims who take a selfless persona seriously, and for similar reasons, even dress like the east with head scarfs and what not".

"Now we know that racism must be wrong, not just is, or could be, so we shouldn't have superiority, it can win, if all will become equal one day in this regard between the races."

"The Ku Klux Clan and its supporters as well as racist right-wingers, like the EDL in Britain once were, off and on, not all the right-wing, have been proved wrong. There is no superiority if we are all moving, primary, to selfless. That's how to remove all abnormal and wired stereotypes from our departure lounge, because we have to stay, stay firm, and relentless towards this goal – proper"! Not lengthily.

"_Ab_normal means we _can_ do or act better or different but don't in disguise which is worse if we become it later unconsciously like Buddhism says if we try and rook here, so be straight, not just normal, by practising."

It is all here, she smiles.

Past western battles were a no way out perception which can weaken now that politics has been conquered and liberated according to recent work on You-Valuism, Paula warns happily.

So get trim, the West, and win.

She says gladly!

LOVE of Sangha-West

(SNIPPET 4)

Some western, white, Sangha members have asked for caring more than curing because the former, they say, helps the latter anyway, a good advice bit. But no one knows why the west's lineage cure anyway. It is because they care – kind not hard, because they are loving. Love cures, they say, but no more so than people without a wrong care in the world. And they hold it, that way, for the betterment of everyone's sake. So, a special thanks to the western Sangha (order of Buddhists monks and nuns) who cured me carefully with wisdom and grace, divine, Paula says, even if actual teachings sometimes falter over time. Not sadly, because it works. Strong, with loving care!

The hope of South Asia

(ARTICLE 30)

…..And Buddhism isn't the only thing that offers hopefulness from South Asia, either, because You-Valuism does not falter too even if it is brimmed with missed hope for some because they feel weaker, it can make people more stable, fit and lean, and it will – soon, approximately 7000 years from now, if true hereonin from 2017, unless people subside into non-existence which they shouldn't if they follow the path - fair.

You-Valuism was born in Sri Lanka, from Britain, and accentuates the idea of Marxism, the Targetter, which is for everyone, Paula insists. How we have to target selflessness anyway if we want You-Valuism, a step after Socialism or Communism, which renders targeting solely for the purpose of betterment intrinsic to capacity-building, because it has to happen for Socialism as well if we pick it.

All this type of targeting is to bring us to One, a common pick, so our multiverse can eventually become its true, deeper universe if we allow, because there is no dodging Saintly Souls as the outcome for every being sooner rather than ages from now, and South Asia is the nearest to that – proved!

But the others don't lag far behind. They are on their way 2.

So get there soon, because multiverse means, in my opinion, Paula says without hybrid intention, many goals, sometimes, competing as the outcome – Pluralism, but not if all is contained in singularity, which some in the east pertain to: i.e. all rivers are moving towards the sacred sea of - God…..which in human terms means nothing other than Saintliness!

Let's not wander from this treasured win!

South Asia will win it for you!

The end of Sin!

Saintliness is the opposite of Sinliness!

That's where we're heading!

A proper dialectic of a different kind.

Which is: You win the opposite of a negative if it is it so positive!

Once in, you're no longer positive or negative, because you are accomplished!

Let's sing it!

The song of Saintliness – truthfully!

Wow!
Why not, if we don't have to be just that? But can be many things on top, which is a vertical kind of multiverse, not where we are heading, right?

Freedom 'from' co-operation, really?

(ARTICLE 31)

Paula Right has said that there comes a time when after we have mastered the art of co-operation in Marxism that we no longer have to try because we have in-built capacity of it so strong we are free from it in practise and never again have to yearn for it because it is neurologically held within.

This means we are 'co-operation-free' and can spend more time working on or doing similar or other-related things or not but freedom of it has been seen through to completion so we are firm in our conviction that Socialism can triumph, Ms. Right heralds unhardily.

The news comes after repeated historical treatments of Marxism in the reports as unattainable after the collapse of the Soviet Empire so fierce that people everywhere rejected its impulse saying it was unworkable and unreachable.

But now people assume that both Oriental people and South Asians of brown colour who invented Buddhism and claim we should be higher even than Marxism, so selfless, are happier, mainly, now, after the work of Benjamin De Silva, with a global Socialist outlook even if it cannot materialise in their own countries presently.

The fear is that people struggling harder for better value-systems, within, might get angry and sabotage violently attempts at making Socialism real so they, the rest, feel it safer to leave it up to the West to lead it in with a higher military hardware background as the reason.

Especially the top Western leaders: political, economic and military.

Ordinary people might try, but they have to overcome all nasty tendencies if they want it on a personal level, between each other, even without leadership from others. But, to have it systemic, global-wide, we need a strong Western-leadership-ring, with will, throughout the whole of the west-country-remit, to ensure it is stable as the next step soon.

Karl Marx had said that Britain would be the leading true Socialist country from outset, because it can, lead in, and the west, Lenin said, should include it unsurreptitiously overall, primarily, which means - first. Both options are on the horizon now, so let's proceed with more perspectives in the media, world-wide, which support it, Socialism truthful, because it does not need to be capitalism's rival, but its synthesis, fine!

Benjamin De Silva

Re-start anew, not re-try, if too wrong

(SNIPPET 5)

One imaginary Buddhist tale, that didn't hit the headlines or the book market, unseen, is people with power from one class attacking another, then *neme* but now, recently, a modern tale - is telling! It says that a group of by standers who were racist belonging to one clan, wanted to attack another type, unfair. Both had powers to deceive, one nicely, the other horrid. So, the first kind, set up an incident, because they had telepathic powers also, where they showed that previously discredited skin-colours, were learning from what the Buddha taught earlier. However, they disguised themselves in multi-cultural ways to act like they were giving happiness to each other, which is what is Buddha's teach. They lied, to impress, and kill later. The Buddha spotted this, and smiled. He knew they were re-trying old habits, and warned them to *restart* something new instead. They did, and helped his Socialist and world peace quest! They were freed!

FREEDOM FROM POLITICS

(ARTICLE 32)

The South Asian community, in one meditation, says it wants, now, freedom from the political ring if all else has been explained from Benjamin De Silva's work, even if we must do other things to achieve perfect balance, can do!

Colonies of past where governed by invaders, but in modern times, more compliant. Post-colonialism takes the form of outside interference in whatever way, even political not just economically so, and, surprisingly, perhaps, psychic, and power-built, Buddhistic, but what is different, in the eyes of South Asians, is, that they want freedom of a particular kind – looks like!

When the "individual" no longer has to be a political animal, something Karl Marx said was inevitable in the current make-up, and it is so, frequently, not just in the polity.

Pauls Right explains: No one now is devoid of capitalism, so we are compelled everywhere to make a stand until all is through, strong and resilient! So we are political, by the nature of the environment, so get with it.

Environmental analysis is different from conditional analysis but both whither in antagonism, politically, when all is equalised to grace – value-wise!

South Asians now know about the "Freedom as capacity" motto, so be in, in to a better climate of the non-political when we have surpassed the selfish mode of capitalism through. Selflessness is higher, as is a fairer world. But, Socialist co-operation can suffice if that's all we need, Paula harps!

As explained before, Paula warns, is this tendency to fruition so that we are free so the two coincide of it, and no more politics.

The freedom *of* politics is not free, really. When we have surpassed it, and need it no more, then we can truly be freer. So, we can see, strong, that Karl Marx was right. When everyone is co-operative-free, as we said in the previous page, that also warrants it – no more politics unfair.

Only kindly.

So get there!

The path of You-Valuism is the way, the way to a higher love and freedom where all surpasses the capitalist systemic syndrome and we reach little politics in – the Buddhist value-system which, as touched on just now, is a kind of selflessness resting on Compassion! Help or Harm?, where we veer on the side of now helping, a step up.

When the whole world is Buddhist in tone, not in religion or theory, necessarily, then all of politics will go except of the semblance of it hanging on where needed but not violently only as when ideas clash, which is the idea of "The Speech" held true.

The real Lion King no longer fights with its claws but can compensate with a kindlier form of politics where we don't care or worry about disdain or inactioning because we all care and can speak to each other instead of, again, clash violently – the end of war!

Paula Right continues that political-peace cannot be, as now, misusing each other for an advantage but is, specifically, about psychological, material and experiential well-being, so nothing should stop us running in that direction firm until all is blissful and worth it for everyone not just ourselves.

It will come.

Go on!

ADVICE TO DOCTORS ON DEATHLESS

(ARTICLE 33)

The death murderers of the health field can change into something less sombre: The lovers of life, eternal or better everlasting health and nothing sad - ideal!

The concept of the Deathless is to "not die" not "live on" a subtle difference which makes the health experts think in a radically different way, innovative, rather than on the spot largely.

Including GPs, hospital staff and mental health clientele.

Paula Right warns: "Nothing is permanent unless we can overcome temporary episodes revolving around what is good – and health is one of them now!

The only heavenly options we have are Hinduism, Christianity at centre and, more lately, Buddhism with The Deathless, if it can work, Paula remarks.

We have to target it: Ongoing health so good that nothing can stop us including death!

Well, that is a heaven option beyond belief, isn't it, if we can win – The Timeless, which we went over not so far ago, for instance making Health the top priority in every field until, over life episodes, we can even say if it is true, no more death beckons.

Why worry? If it is in. We just have to go through to it, regardless of how long it takes, with conviction, until it lasts, a no ditch effort geared toward no ill health ever again.

Dismayed? Well, we thought the idea of ongoing life was a mystery, but now it can be in.

"The terrible state of doctors surgeries and their unhelpful staff has always been a nightmare for many, even as they complain about overwork which a Socialist society would reduce pliantly until it is a breeze for everyone who is not physically despaired."

In war-zones it is even worse if held covert. "I once heard of health staff in an underdeveloped country working in a military capacity. If true, hope not, how deep, and wide, which countries, if any, including in modern, does this problem subside?, Paula asks.

We have a long way to go, Paula warrants.
The terrible state of our mental health systems in every
country can vanquish when we target properly, not on money
and business success – or militarily – if in some places, but
moral, and, I might, spiritual, goals, heartfelt until we win –
The Deathless itself.
It can work!
Doctors – go for it!

Liberation Verses Freedom

(SNIPPET 6)

There is a confusion. What is liberation and why is it classed a type or kind of freedom in its own regard? Well, the truth is, I see, that the former, Liberation, is when someone else does it for you, like Martin Luther King did it for us, whereas the latter, Freedom, is when it's done yourself as in the "pursuit" of freedom in the American constitution therein. Hope it unhells! Please do!

Socialism in One Country?

(ARTICLE 34)

Some say, like Cuba, it's ok to have Socialism, a Communist pick, in a country even if others don't subdue to it. Others say, it has to be global. But we say, it's ok to have it in one, like Britain, true Socialism, then, if, and only if, it can _spread_ – fairly – to all other places atrue.

Paula stacks up: "The problem is people have argued along these lines for far too long and it must end – Now! What is better, is to get started. Once REAL Socialism is established in say Britain, out of the capitalist system, finally, in envisionment, then we can muster enough courage to go to other SAFE places."

This must happen, within the next 60 years or so from nowonin.

Within Britain.

The opposition is vast, but now the parameters have been drawn: It's a steady path up to Compassion in all religions, starting with the political and economic system, for all – everyone!, Paula insists.

So smile, Paula motions.

The "forms" have been laid out clearly at last, we all know we can get there, strong and upright, all we have to do is go gradually and not give in, unobsessively!

We don't' need a delinear reaction where we reject all paths, because this is one, and it is right: 'me', to 'us', to, finally 'you' – You-Valuism itself – selflessness in politics.

Delineation is what few Buddhists have done and it is wrong, because a path-goal linear verdict is strong if we don't cling and are suffering from the actions of others, it can help, not obsessively, but at least strategically – self-conscious! It must. And we converted it to a graded, structural path, for politics, near, and it won!

Paula shouts: "Delineation cannot afford to get into an anti-You-Valuist state it must be avoided because the purpose of path-goal models for us, here, in political theory, is to sidestep the dialectic of conflict often culminating in violent behaviour, and it can work – Pragmatism, if done slow and true."

With this kind of care, with Socialism stacked in, within the system of politics contained in the analysis aimed at, finally, a politics of selflessness everywhere, will-can at last afford to spread its wings and temper into all country-wide climates: steady, fair and lasting!

We need an office of You-Valuism to muster enough strength to "Bud" for Buddha a new political office that can flower generations on like Buddhism until complete, which is when we win – political selflessness and compassion from Buddhism and other religions everywhere!

The western Sangha should realise this is the only way to end all forms of negative dialectics which do exists in society, broad, until it becomes irreversible and all forms of dialectical reasoning have been dissolved for good, replaced by a higher function of the mind similar to The Buddha's which is soft, gentle and still, even in speech!

Let's get there!, until all is solid for those harking on about the past without a care for the present and forward thinking that is productive and careful, this is a must!

Go on!

Do it!

Overcoming murder

(ARTICLE 35)

There are two types of murder we have to be weary of currently: conditional and internal. Fine! If it is intentional, then we are within, a dilemma of internality and how to improve this, so we are free of all mishope and non-care. If murder is based on the conditions we couldn't control, it is equally worryful, but different, because it is outside.

The former renders the need to improve the mental health and integral value of the victim, You-Valuism in scope I see, however the latter now requires additional help from those who can manage it. Vasantha-Raja, for instance, the writer and political commentator, also my father, Paula unwarrants, has helped in this regard. For conditional non-worry, he underscores the need for a Universal Welfare State (UWS) to make life manageable and non-murderous like not swapping the dole or feeble benefits funds as governments change, so, he says, the welfare state can and must be, instead: "fully-fledged" not "half-baked" to accommodate everyone, even if criminal-types for it need to be helped with a community force designed to not let them go for unseen advantage mismanaged and scary – crime itself! True!

I am disgusted, Paula weaves in. Ms Right is astonished that neither the West nor the East has sufficient funds, they claim, to partake in "Futuristic Welfare", a concept she added on to Vasantha-Raja's claim that the money can exist if banks are under the public purse and ownership. Futuristic Welfare is the idea of non-partisan benefits, which means singularity until money, millions of years down the road, vanishes or is dissolved for the Zero, no money but higher systemically, what now (me) Benjamin De Silva describes as Magic Zeroing – fair and upright – smart, as well!

Then, both intentional murder and the conditional type will reduce considerably one hopes, in one sense at least, so be clean, steady and good, and get there soon, so we can live on happily between each other – not just within! – with added value, not added murder – free!

Police be weary

(Snippet 7)

The global police are up against a formidable task with the hell-bent public, largely, not wholly, who have a history of attacking leaders even though they are benefiting from them, instead of steering them gracefully to better agendas if need be – firm not disgraceful!

Paula added: "This is what you (the police) are up against with more light at the end of the tunnel now, thankfully for us, we have proven that value counts and we are made largely over Karma partly due to the value we bring, including what group of peoples we are born into, primarily, perhaps".

Because when all is equal, we won't need to care about colour because it stinks that we care only about which group or skin-colour we belong to, which some have overcome, including me, Paula warns.

She warned the police that "despite giving immensely more than many in intellectual capacity and worth, including vision for everlasting life; rationality without suffering in the mind; a path to no more violence in politics, clarity of thought, easy understanding and much more, not one person in public, perhaps only a few, have even said the word "Thank You"!

This is what you face, she said to policemen and women coppishly!, however good you are or intend to be for their benefit even unconditionally – how sad!

With some, lashing out verbal and actioning violence "for more" regardless of how much you have given to them in past battles on their behalf with moral conduct in-tact ongoing – and generously with fair added on! ABUSE!

Another strategising effort to "abuse" is when the public "fight" on behalf of the leader unwantedly to jeopardise things by doing it falsely. Police, please be aware of this strategy.

Non-Violence & Socialism

(ARTICLE 36)

Police-Monks working, hand-in-hand, is possible if both take on the anti-murder, anti-suicide newer form of my version of Buddhism, even if other layerings already contained within the religion therein should be kept zealously for everyone always - from hereonin!

This means we protect people from murder and attack as the basis of this and other religions, at ideal, and never give in, with our safety kept intact – ongoing.

Socialism should follow!

Paula Right warrants: "There is no scope for violence in Socialism unless there is no hope and oppression uncontrolled against you and to your death which is rare historically unless pitted in war which has now been removed theoretically – altogether!" With You-Valuism – fair, not square!

"Ahimsa is the Ghandian concept of Non-Violence and it should never end if we now know that all we need is value-enhancement in politics until all we require is "speech" and "talk" like Lion Kings who roar rather than act ferociously to others' devastation, who guard not attack defensively – a point, in hand. Why? Because that's how Ghandi was offensive, with the – GUARD SPIRIT – well-known sometimes in sport."

Defenders, football, often attack unilaterally, like goal-keepers, bizarre and outspoken in action, but clever, which is what the South Asian attack is – its defensive, not in the negative, but sporty, to the win – clever, yet again, and it won independence, so others learn if it is just a few value-steps away, with practise, eventually effortlessly, but strong!

Not alone, walk ever on!

So Socialism should be the same, and the army concept of the workers – fair, not abusive, can win it for the west also if others try a return for Colonialism gone wrong, which must end in covert ways too once all is clear and everyone sees that Socialism is still on the cards, fully, and not weakly, but cleverly, and self-righteously. Hurrah!

Re-introduced by server, Benjamin De Silva - he even calls himself "The Helper-Servant" - for returning Marxism back to its rightful place as the only way to end the standoff between different races without having full-blown Socialism until it is ready - which is soon!
Let's close!
Be peaceful!

FASCISM & UGLINESS

(ARTICLE 37)

The problem of disfigurement or ugliness is so deep-rooted in society it was a core part of the Fascist ideology in Nazi Germany during World War II, but it doesn't have to be, Paula said, after being incited about it at BBC World many years ago. Asian Times, a then part of ethic media group, where she worked (alias), also suffered the same fate, once upon a time, at least – frank! How widespread is it in journalism and other fields, the problem of poor looks?

Do they want better husbands and wives, did they act violently to others in a past life with a "laughing at them" mentality to suffer the same indecency in physical appearance as the Karma knock later? The Fascists didn't know, but we did, including the Buddhists in London and elsewhere who say "unkindness" to others is what brings it on later, the next life over, which giggling at killing or harming others is – unkind, she said softly.

The BBC pointed the behaviour out, as if it happened in politics, too, behind closed scenes, which it resembles when people laugh uglily even in a context like war which is tremendously unpowerful really, if we get kicked by Karma anyway to ourselves by an _objective_ law which is superior to human intent now truly, isn't it?

But, in any case, now, we know that is, the Fascists were wrong if they held their rationality subjectively instead of seeing Karma as the cause, not the denial by opponents of the need to portray for achievement through science a super-human race, whether it had blonde hair or blue eyes or not, well, isn't it? No? No, right. Because all you have to do is be kind ongoing until it flirts in better physical structure through the law of moral causation outside us not within.

So get there steady, for a precious appearance, over life episodes, and it will win, if both material and mental reality can move ahead, pliantly, towards a greater freedom in physical looks and mental suffering, like Benjamin De Silva wants!

UNTV

(ARTICLE 38)
Paula Right has called for a new television news channel and audience for a conflict resolution network based at the United Nations in New York and headed by a top journalist with severe experience of war and conflict even within states like the most-respected Jon Snow who is the senior presenter at Channel 4 News in London as its HQ, but only if he thinks it's good and deserved of his talents. Right!!! Not otherwise!
The Politics Of Right in Kant means we can see the evil, wrongness or worry in interpretation, even fallacious reasoning, and subsidise it with correct view which is Right, again, the politic of right in Kant, explained!
And the UNTV idea is one of these tendencies even! True?
Paula Right explains: "We have to much worry on "what happens" in war which is feeble, we need to strike harder at the cessation point, again, seeing the ending of things, an idea in Buddhism, which is neat, like the ending of all conflict and, therefore, peace world-wide."
And it can happen in media.
Even a small paper like Asian Times, which Ishara edited, for South Asia's brown community in the UK, struck out in Northern Ireland and won, all with the help of the police and global media TV networks, mainly, and investigation techniques of the editor he was then, not now, he is an author. ISHARA called for a 'One Country, Two Nations' solution type for the then ethic conflict in Sri Lanka, also and Ireland, again, to repeat, which accommodated both sides of the warring factions in each residue of war that was torn in the two countries and it won, an assignment Ishara's father gave to him when young as the first step to finding peace in Sri Lanka first, that is, as a 'problem-solver'!
He did, and Jon Snow helped, openly and non-violently.
So he should be picked to voluntarily _head_ a prospective UNTV project if it is an agenda he likes, not otherwise, I stand.

Benjamin De Silva

THE AVATAR: So what is it – really?

(SNIPPET 8)

Some people say, definitively, that an Avatar is the teacher of the "No-Soul" concept in eastern religion where soul is defined as "The Atman". Well we say 'no'. The Avatar is a "teacher of religious folk and institutions" I think, like the Buddha is, to this day, and people resemble and respect him everywhere as a true teacher of religiosity! So get there, everyone interested in religious studies. I want to, and will, soon, exclaims Paula!

Falsify war, not verify it!

(SNIPPET 9)

The peoples of the world should find a way to solve all combatants not justify wars for their own ends or evil, Paula Right explains.

The one-time editor said we shouldn't find ways of seeking war, or more of it, but _falsify_, strong, its wrong or wrongness non-abruptly, but fair!

This is the end, the end of now world-placed-wars, eventually, when we win – fairness for the peoples of the world at last without worry only non-worry right the way through, in line with Karma, then, agreeably! For ourselves and others in tune, in tune with the universe and its making.

Benjamin De Silva

A Meditation Focus

(SNIPPET 9)

A criminal opened up to me today remarking that what they need is "mothers" not just "fathers" as in the father of the Lord or religious folk. Maybe a significant number of South Asian mothers, or top-value females, should put journalistic writing regular together in the guise of "mothers" to them, and falsify the idea, rightly, and eventually only, in other professions also, to make them strong soon! Focus hard on my suggestion mum. Paula.

Import-Substitute "Socialism", not industrialisation

(SNIPPET 10)

Britain can be first to Socialism and if other countries don't correspond they can substitute Socialism with trade: import and export, with domestic relations fully Socialist, as that would be great when an advanced country such as the UK is mainly a Socialist one until fully there world-wide.

This is both 'import-substitution Socialism' and 'export-substitution Socialism' until true socialism is complete throughout the world - fair! Like Karma.

This is in contrast to other systems of substitution for both forms of trading known as 'industrial' forms to cover up, looks like, capitalism in disguise but in a different manner for the heartache many express about the system unpopular.

Psychological Thirst!

(ARTICLE 39)

Sometimes when we thirst for things we get lost, but nothing knows why when we get thirsty for water, we actually like it, the right way!, says Paula Right, the respected journalist. Buddhists say not to have psychological thirstiness for what we want and they are right because, especially when we're restricted by others in getting there, we lose, and get agitated, so we have to win – strong, Paula smiles.

But it also can be right, Paula laughs.

When I had the thirst for peace in Sri Lanka, I was like a concorde, verging off path, until it or I got there – firm! The end.

So history didn't repeat itself, like the psychologists at St Anne's hospital thought I was doing after I had a schizophrenic breakdown and went for treatment there, Paula giggles.

Everything is an "operation" in success for something better, for me and others, for me, so it can backfire if I get there in then finally, and so it can be with you too, Paula advises.

Especially if you "win" for others, not much heard of in western or eastern societies, even peace within is daunting for ourselves if it doesn't work until free, the emptiness of emptiness is it – deeper levels of peace, not happiness, itself!, for most, a well-known component of Buddhist philosophy now, and then!

But Bodhisattvas, which I want to be, Paula explains, have to do it – win for others, to repeat, yet again, and we did it for people in Sri Lanka, helping to bring peace to the Sinhala-Tamil conflict which the polity organised to defeat an oppressed (they claim) and oppressive force (some say) – the Liberation Tigers Of Tamil Eelam, and it worked, for justice, with all concerned.

But with that, has come the onset of another tempering conflict, this time between the Buddhists and Muslims, especially one Buddhist group labelled by western media as "Fascists", so we should help there too, if Sri Lanka is where I originate from, Paula laughs out loud. But we should understand the "social structure" of the embattlers as well as the region to see the relationships and, therefore, the

dynamics, which keep it in play, for better analysis all-round, especially for the Sri Lankans themselves.
So keep on trying, and we'll get there, without hell-bent thirst, psychological, only a kindlier one, good and proper!
It can win!

Benjamin De Silva

GENDER AND MARXISM

(ARTICLE 40)

Rosa Luxemburg wanted a fairer Marxism and got stuck in an attic with her work, always mistrusting the Marxists of her age spying on them to see if there is a better deal for women, a fear still prevalent in modern times among many Socialists of their type – uncanny!

Paula Right continues the tradition but instead says there is a simple answer: To value yourself and not care if others improve even if you need them to muster greater strength to lift-off for a better world between the two classes, man and woman, a gender gap unfree presently but not ongoing or, unbetter, not forever!

Paula insists: "Take your time, don't rush, because all is not lost, we have to win freely, and it's not in others' power to stop you, stop you from becoming free, because gender equality is based, again, on value, which is currently a selfish 'me' in capitalism".

A dubious drive, she repeats frankly.

Although the idea that women are more caring than men is not always true, the reason for falter is not this, but that we were in disguise, not knowing ourself, true realisation, our true nature, she hints.

"We have to strive for better, and make it work, the real self is our essence which under capitalism is selfishly geared, for women as well, so strive harder, for more, not more accumulation, but more worth, self-worth," she speaks earnestly and truthfully, even if repeatedly.

The gender worry has taken many centuries to fulfil and we are still lost in words, the acclaimed author spoke, this needs to change fast and vehemently for a brighter world to materialise.

In the distant past, we had to survive, as cave-people now, not men, but in this era, there is still hope for equality between the sexes, but it is a gradual process, she remarks.

Political ideology and sex equality collide as well as converge and they do so, the latter, on: nearly last time, VALUE.

This value is the shift from "Capitalist greed" to "Socialist co-operation", targeted freely with a Marxist bent, she said finally.

When both men and women achieve this, an equal eye between the two will be seen, she insists, as self-worth inter-related with each sex harnesses triumphantly.

Giving to your mother

(ARTICLE 41)

The Buddhist word 'Paramitas' seems to stems from the concept of 'Parameter' which means here the guidelines for developing your character, says Paula.

Mum was asking, no preying, that her abilities will improve so she can reap a better quality of life in this world where people misuse and attack for no reason whatsoever except hell-bent, which can be transcended, oh no I gave it away, Paula smiles. So, she informed her that the reason for guidance is so we "improve" and the way to do it is set out in the You-Valuism philosophy, no political philosophy, which says we have to enhance our value in one way: from none, me, us, to you. Or, in other words, best suited from fascism of past wars and havoc, capitalism of own gain, socialism of self-serving-others, and, finally, to You-Valuism of No-Self by giving outwardly – the art of Compassion!

Mum was scared, but I informed her that all this requires is to set yourself goals so that you win improvement of the Buddhist Paramitas, where these values – none 2 you – are the Parameters.

The Paramitas are:

1. Generosity (dana)
2. Moral conduct (sila)
3. Renunciation (nekkhamma)
4. Wisdom (paññā)
5. Energy (viriya)
6. Patience (khanti)
7. Truthfulness (sacca)
8. Determination (adhitthana)
9. Loving-kindness (metta)
10. Equanimity (upekkha)

So, that says it, Paula laughs.

"All there is, is this, if you want to get higher on earth and receive better from yourself and when others do it, too, then there will be peace on earth, not just your own win." Existentialism, to capitalism, to socialism to you-valuism is the marked step upgrade which we have to sail past until complete, so take it on the chin mum, Paula said, and plan wisely for this, whatever else you do, be yourself, and pick other goals in tandem.

So, Paula's mum was given a blessing by Buddhism. Her prayer had been answered. She could finally find a sure way to achieve her hopes, to live cleverly and wisely and lead a better life when nothing else would let her live, peacefully.

I explained to her that it was just because of the stage we were at in life and Earth-life to be precise in the Karma context, so that people were still grappling with their past Karma, Paula envisioned.

These, the Parameters and Paramitas, will, I hope, make people wiser after its large insight to weave through life more kindly, she said willingly.

I knew my mum had won from me at last!, she said patiently. Then there was silence!

Is war worth it? No

(ARTICLE 42)

The pride of the family was at stake once we said our agenda for life was, primarily, even if not only, the non-gambit of World Peace itself. And it won, partly.

We have now discovered what the value-system is for: to guide men and women to no more war on Earth as compassionate beings prepared to help one and other in need – and it has stuck, for many, even if not all!

The parameters are clear: stage 1 to stage 4, and many of us are near, which all can be when we muster the strength to live freely within the remit of no more harm – so harmless!

But many still subside in a war mentality, even unofficially. And it stinks, Paula Right warranted.

"The greatest tragedy is war, and those who think it is worth it, haven't understood the idea of 'value' yet until it springs greater satisfaction the world over. But we must start, vehemently. And it will materialise better for everyone – lasting!" All they need is love.

From Fire 2 Wind

(SNIPPET 11)

So far, everyone seems to be fighting fire with fire, attacking harsh even in non-war-zones near it though even in the west, which is – fire - the dominant element well-known in astrology for most. But we are trying to turn it into wind, where people speak solutions or shout them, using verbal language instead of fists or guns/bombs, or violent-type strategies. Wind, not fire, then. Please! Now. Full on. With truth! Here, and now, everywhere, everyone! This is the cure for all! True say!

The Criminal Mind!

(ARTICLE 43)

Paula yelled. This has to stop. All the people around her and from her past started strategizing for her out of greed for what she could give them, and it didn't work, after she made some progress with Buddhism and meditation, when she was, earlier, seen as "nothing", fit for nothing whatsoever!

But Paula worked out, after analysing their movements that there was more to The Criminal Mind than strategizing, there was, for some of them, contained in it a "re" element, namely _re-strategising_, for something more in one way or another.

So, this is the criminal mind, again, in some...and some ways. Some of their ideas in Paula's interpretation of them, are: Planning to win something for you when they didn't before fully so as to give the impression they have helped you so they are entitled to receive from you afterwards. Then, _restrategising_ after failure in this - making you look weird to bewilder you and take, a freakish strategy, if they have become freaks, psychologically, through abnormal behaviour, on a slant, themselves, perhaps, as the cause – if crime is seen as science, she thought.

Then, if that fails, making life "shit" for you if it's already good, why?, to make you suffer for not giving anything or more to them – crime – and, in the attack, hoping you will do it, give them something worthwhile, after. Then, if failed, only giving you something you like if you're going to give them something they like, not what you offer, what a mentality, Paula yawned.

Then, if all else fails, recording you on the phone, and giving off the noise of gun pistols to scare, as if you are not the good one, this time done more powerfully in greed to get much more things, now, not over time once your (Paula's) capabilities are known further.

These are just some cases, a re-strategising formula in, all coiled in – or, combined. Many more exist, phoney!

All wrong and hell-bent.

Sad!

Let's hope it never wins within anyone, Paula exclaimed!

Karma-Decisioning Mum

(SNIPPET 12)

Mum made a blunder, Paula explains. She allowed the lack of love from others to make her feel restricted, and thereby let herself roll-back into ineptitude. This is what happens first when we make an error in advance for forward actioning gone all wrong, we see no option when there is. Because we feel let down.

But don't falter, she said. Because when we keep an eye on Karma law, we make decisions that fit it and keep us strong, stronger than otherwise, which is known as "Karma-decisioning". So do it mum, Paula yelled to her. Keep fit, fit with Karmaring, so ride Karma well, was her message. And it stuck. Mum never faltered this way again, she hopes.

Buddhism & The Dole

(ARTICLE 44)

People, not criminals, on the dole are often treated as crime, not by all, but by some! Paula yawned, again, fearlessly now! Just figures.

But WHAT IF....Buddhists, the monks and nuns, were allowed significant proportions of wealth by national governments to cater for their survival and well-being, what will it bring – WOW!?

This is what I recommend!

Paula adds: "There is too much scope beyond capitalism that it is weak to remain solely on a donation model when we're "stuck" on a donational model for the Buddhists, not all, but the priests."

"This must end".

"Why"?

"Because, the time has come for a socialist end where money isn't an obstacle to wealth but a vehicle for it, in abundance, which a You-Valuist model, afterwards, will win not scorn unlimited wealth for all, we assume: gradually, patiently and without shock, one day for all whatever our value (good) – when all is free and giving, selflessly".

But, before then, the Universal Welfare State idea will be kind to Buddhism also, in perception first, then in reality, we hope, so that the Buddhist community don't have to be scorned to accept capitalism but can strive for more with welfare help unconditional like it brings.

"This is the start of Socialism".

Paula is humble.

How to change the world!

(ARTICLE 49)

They say to change the world you have to understand it first so led by enlightened people upfront. Others say, like Marxists of old you have to change the system hell-bent. The truth is something different.

Yes, you have to change yourself. But, in a very specific way: *By uplifting your value scale!*

From: no-value, to me-value, to us-value, to, finally, you-value (selflessness), the climax which is You-Valuism itself when you're in, with it within you – strong!

Benjamin De Silva

In Love Of My Father

This book is dedicated in addition to my father who encouraged his children throughout his life to change the world for the betterment of mankind and this book is part of that project.

It is with love to him that this book is offered with no small regard for his huge contribution to the world by making all separatist and self-determination movements world-wide conducive to a world peace agenda that warrants greater prosperity to everyone not just the privileged few.

It is because of him that this book was written on behalf of all those wishing that peace will come to mankind, people from all communities: Black, White, Oriental & Brown! It is to all of these that my wishes for a more loving world is given. May these blessings live on for eternity until we reach The Deathless – Everlasting Life produced by Excellence in Health Studies throughout the world forever on!

Good wishes!

www.ingramcontent.com/pod-product-compliance
Lightning Source LLC
Chambersburg PA
CBHW040254290326
41929CB00051B/3376